Percy Thrower's
How to Grow
Vegetables and Fruit

Percy Thrower's
How to Grow
Vegetables
and Fruit

TREASURE PRESS

ACKNOWLEDGEMENTS

The publishers would like to thank the following for
the photographs used in this book:
Amateur Gardening, Pat Brindley, Robert Corbin,
John Cowley, Valerie Finnis, Brian Furner, Robert
Pearson, Ray Procter, Harry Smith Horticultural
Collection, and Suttons Seeds

Line and colour artwork by The Hayward Art Group

First published in Great Britain in 1977 by
The Hamlyn Publishing Group Limited

This edition published in 1987 by
Treasure Press
59 Grosvenor Street
London W1

ISBN 1 85051 239 6

Printed in Hong Kong

Contents

Growing Vegetables 10

Growing Fruit 74

Index 124

Growing Vegetables

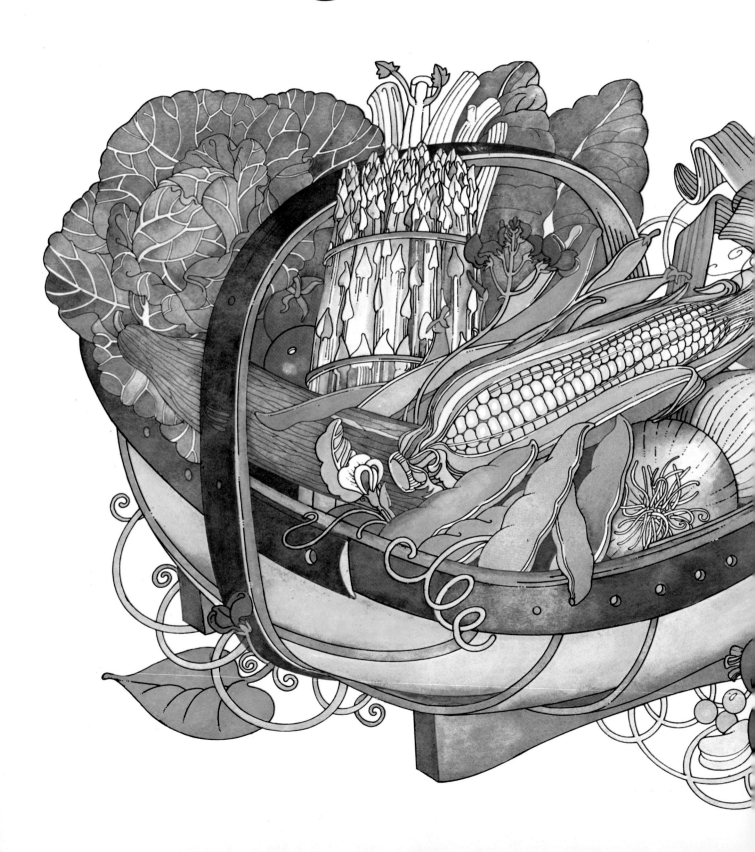

Vegetables have three main requirements – sun, good soil and enough water. It is a mistake to think that they can be tucked away under trees or in the shade of walls or buildings; in such positions the resulting crops may well be unpalatable and will almost certainly be uneconomic.

The secret of growing vegetables that can be brought with pride to the table is to grow them quickly, making sure that they suffer no check to their growth through shortage of water and lack of food. So when selecting a site, choose an open, light position and prepare the soil well.

must, necessarily, depend on a number of factors. First, the family's likes and dislikes – there is no point in having a plentiful supply of spinach, for example, if no one can be persuaded to touch it. The second factor which may affect the decision for a large number of gardeners is the type of soil, it is no good trying to grow parsnips in stony soil, nor will such crops as runner beans, summer spinach, radishes, peas and lettuces succeed in fast-draining light soil unless measures are taken to improve it.

The size of the area available is another consideration, but even the smallest plot can be put to some use; in fact, I have seen many gardens where vegetables such as lettuces, radishes, and runner beans are grown in the flower border.

In small gardens the best idea is to concentrate on the quicker maturing crops, early salads, and those which give a good return because they are high yielding.

Recommended crops for a small garden. Lettuce, radish, carrots, spring onions, beetroot, runner beans,

Growing vegetables in containers

I always think that one of the attractions of vegetable growing is that it is not limited to those with a garden, worthwhile crops can be taken from vegetables grown in pots, window boxes, raised beds, or the very useful peat bags. And a selection of these can be accommodated on any reasonably sized balcony or patio.

For growing in pots and window boxes I recommend as a growing medium either John Innes potting compost No. 3 or one of the peat-based composts. The peat bags come ready filled with a specially formulated growing medium – and very good it is too. The important thing to remember with regard to vegetables grown in containers is the need for regular watering and feeding, such plants have less reserves to draw on than those grown in the open ground.

Recommended crops. There is really no limit to the sort of crops which can be grown in containers but I suggest that you concentrate on some of the higher yielding kinds. Runner and French beans, marrows, tomatoes, potatoes, and broccoli, are some that come to mind. Certain crops often do better in containers, pepper and aubergines are examples of these. And do not forget the herbs. These, freshly picked, make all the difference to many culinary dishes and it is easy to keep a supply available in pots placed conveniently outside the kitchen door.

Planning the vegetable garden

The first priority in planning the vegetable garden is to decide what crops to grow so that the seed can be ordered as early in the year as possible. This decision

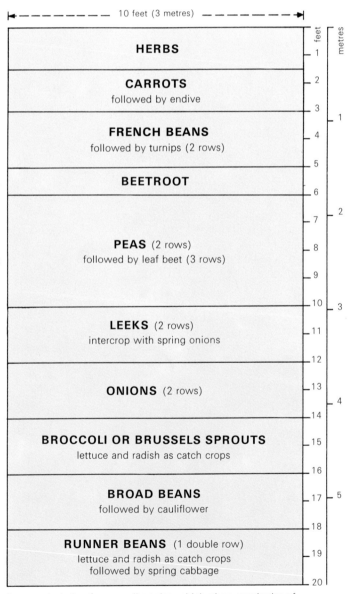

A suggested plan for a small garden which gives continuity of cropping and a useful range of vegetables

broad beans, peas, and spinach, with broccoli, cabbage, leaf beet, leeks and endive to follow.

Choosing varieties

There is such a wide choice of varieties available from various seed firms that it is often a puzzle to know which to grow. I have made some suggestions in the text under each crop but I would also advise you to talk to other local gardeners and find out what varieties do well in your area.

Making the most of your vegetable garden

In these days of high-priced vegetables how important it is to get the maximum value from each vegetable grown by finding ways of producing crops early when they are at their most expensive, by growing only as much as you can use at any one time, and by never allowing any area of ground to stand idle.

Using cloches, frames and green-houses

In this country by providing some form of protection either early or late in the year, it is perfectly feasible to encourage certain vegetables to crop up to a month ahead of their normal season. Cloches, in particular, will soon pay for their keep when used to protect early outdoor sowings, or to warm the soil and so allow crops such as French and runner beans to be sown earlier than would normally be possible. They do not need to be expensive: I use the corrugated plastic ones but the tunnel sort made from plastic sheeting are equally effective.

Garden frames, apart from being used later in the season for raising melons and frame cucumbers, provide protection in the earlier stages for pot- or box-sown seeds, and for hardening off seedlings once they have been pricked out. If the frame is heated, so much the better, but this is not necessary.

The heated greenhouse, while offering the best protection and the best chance of getting plants off to a good start is also expensive to run, and this must be taken into account when working out its value. In the long run, you may consider it more economic to buy seedling plants from the nursery or garden centre and not attempt to raise them yourself.

Unheated greenhouses can be used for seed sowings from February to April and are ideal for growing such crops as tomatoes, early lettuce, peppers, aubergines, early beans in pots and early potatoes in pots.

Successional sowing

This term is used for one of the most important rules in vegetable growing – that of sowing small quantities of seed at intervals of two to three weeks instead of the whole lot at one go. In this way the crop is evened out and can be picked in manageable quantities. A great many of the summer vegetables will not stand long once they are ready for harvesting and if there are more than are needed then the results are rows of bolting lettuces and spinach, tough unpalatable radishes, stringy root crops or a glut of marrows, to name but a few. So make a point of sowing only a quarter to half a row at a time, or in the case of individual seed sowings, such as those of marrow, spread them over a period of three weeks or so.

Catch cropping and intercropping

These are techniques which, although essentially simple, come more easily with practice. By using them you will make sure that the ground is cropped to its full capacity.

Catch cropping refers to the practice of growing quick-maturing crops on ground which is reserved for later sown crops such as the brassicas or which has been used for an early crop such as peas or broad beans. Turnips, swedes, radish and lettuces are all suitable for this purpose.

Intercropping is a variation on catch cropping in which quick-maturing vegetables are sown between the rows of long-term ones in the knowledge that they will have produced their crop and be off the ground before it is needed by the expanding growth of the main crops. Some examples of this are lettuce and radish sown between celery, spring onions and lettuce sown between broccoli and cauliflower, and lettuce, radish and spinach sown between peas and broad beans.

Crop rotation

Where sufficient space is available it is inadvisable for any vegetable to be grown on the same piece of ground two years running. There are two main reasons

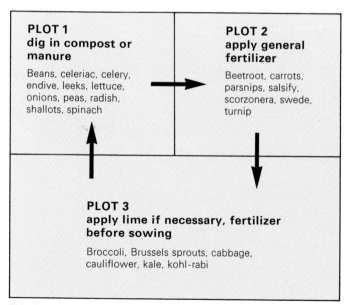

This diagram illustrates the principle of crop rotation in which the vegetables are moved to a different site each year

for this. The first is that different crops have different food requirements and so take different amounts of food from the soil. Therefore by moving the crops around the soil is not depleted.

The second reason is that it discourages the build-up of serious pests and diseases which are linked to particular vegetables. For example, club root disease which affects brassicas, white rot of onions and potato root eelworm.

There are several ways of carrying out crop rotation; the one most frequently used is to divide the ground into three equal areas and the vegetables into three groups. Each area of ground is treated differently with regard to feeding and manuring and each group of vegetables is grown on the ground which has had the most suitable treatment for that group. Then in the next two successive years the crops are rotated so that each group of vegetables is grown in each area only once every three years.

In small gardens such a complicated system of rotation is clearly both impossible and unnecessary where the range of crops grown is small, and even in bigger gardens you may not wish to devote an equal amount of space to each of the various groups. Here, I suggest that you plan a system which will work for you – bearing in mind the fact that you should try to change the position of each vegetable every year.

A compost heap should be a permanent feature of the vegetable garden. There are various ways of containing the heap and rigid plastic netting makes an easy surround

organic matter is most effective if dug in only a month or six weeks before seed sowing.

I am fortunate in having good soil in my own vegetable garden and I like to keep it that way by digging it in the autumn to a depth of at least 25 cm (10 in) – in a large area this is less back breaking if a cultivator is used – and incorporating organic matter into one-third of the plot each year.

Soil preparation

This is, I think, the biggest single factor in successful vegetable production. A well-prepared soil with a good content of humus-forming organic matter is naturally moisture retentive as well as containing a supply of the necessary nutrients.

Few of us start with an ideal soil – one that is friable and moisture-retentive yet well drained. Instead we have to battle with either heavy clay, which tends to be waterlogged in winter and slow to warm up in spring making it useful only for summer and autumn crops, or a light sandy soil which, although quick to warm up, is free draining and so no use for summer crops.

Fortunately much can be done to improve the soil by good cultivating and adding some form of bulky organic matter with additional dressings of lime and fertilizers where necessary.

The site for the vegetable garden should be dug during the autumn and winter and the surface of the soil left rough so that the lumps can be broken down by frost action. This is especially important in the case of clay soils but, as these become difficult to work in wet weather, the digging should be done as early as possible in the autumn. At the same time some form of well-rotted organic matter – farmyard manure, garden compost, spent mushroom compost – should be worked in. This will help to break up the clay particles and so get more air into the soil and allow excess water to drain away.

Light, quick-draining soil is also much improved by the addition of organic matter. In this case the

Garden compost

The compost heap is the easiest way of maintaining a constant supply of organic matter for use in the garden. All materials of a vegetable origin will eventually decay but avoid including the roots of perennial weeds, pest- or disease-ridden plants, and woody materials which will take a lot of time to rot.

The rate of decay can be encouraged by using an accelerating chemical between every 23-cm (9-in) layer of refuse material. Proprietary compost accelerators are available, or you can use Nitro-chalk. Moisten any dry material used in the heap and turn the heap after about six weeks, bringing the inner part to the outside.

Fertilizers

Bulky organic matter is an essential ingredient for improving soil texture but I also use chemical fertilizers to ensure that the plants obtain all the food they need.

The most important plant foods are nitrogen, phosphorus and potassium, and a number of others, including magnesium, iron and manganese, are required in much smaller quantities. It is perhaps useful to look at the role of the three main foods in the life of the plant.

Nitrogen encourages good colour and vigorous growth and so is particularly useful for the leafy crops – spinach, cabbage, lettuce.

Phosphorus is necessary for good root growth and

helps seedlings and young plants to get off to a good start. It follows from this that this is one of the most important foods for the root crops.

Potassium helps to produce disease-resistant plants with strong stems, but it is particularly important for its effect on the size and colour of fruit and vegetables, encouraging as it does fruitfulness and speed of ripening.

These chemicals are available in various ready mixed forms and this is the easiest way to use them because the mixing has been done to give the correct balance of chemicals for a specific use. For example, tomato fertilizer has a higher potash content which is useful both to this crop and to various other crops, and rose fertilizer as well as a high potash content has some additional chemicals such as magnesium which make it a good choice for use on many of the fruits.

General or all-purpose fertilizers contain almost equal amounts of all three main plant foods and this is the formula with the widest use.

The percentages of the chemicals used in them is shown on the packagings of all ready mixed fertilizers. Nitrogen may be expressed as N, phosphorus as phosphoric acid or P_2O_5, and potassium as potash or K_2O.

The fertilizers just mentioned are all known as inorganic because they are of chemical origin, there is also a range of non-bulky organic manures of animal or vegetable origin which can be used to supply the necessary foods. Dried blood and hoof and horn meal provide nitrogen, bonemeal is a source of phosphoric acid, and wood ash and fish meal are sources of potash. These are also available ready mixed and 'blood, fish and bone' is an excellent general organic fertilizer. The main advantage of the organic fertilizers is that they are not broken down as quickly as the inorganic and so have a longer life in the soil. It also follows, however, that they must be applied some weeks in advance of the time when they will actually be needed.

Fertilizers, as opposed to the bulky organic manures

Vegetables brought fresh to the table from the garden are ample reward for the work involved in growing them

15

Seed sowing out of doors Tread well to firm the soil and then rake to a fine tilth, adding fertilizer if necessary

Sowing seed broadcast is done by scattering it lightly over the surface of the soil and raking it in

Sowing in drills. Using a line as a guide take out a shallow furrow or 'drill' with a hoe or pointed stick

Water the drill and then sow the seeds evenly and thinly to avoid wastage

Fill in the drill by shuffling the soil back with the feet. Label the row with details of the crop and the date

Seedlings are in constant competition for light and food and must be thinned out when they are a couple of inches high

which are dug into the soil or used as mulches, are usually applied as topdressings – being sprinkled on the surface of the soil and lightly raked in.

The value of lime. Lime has two main uses: it helps to counteract acidity, and improves the texture of clay soil. Few vegetables grow well in an acid soil and it is a wise precaution to find out whether your intended plot is acid or alkaline by carrying out a simple test using one of the proprietary soil-testing kits available from garden centres or shops. These will show the degree of acidity and will suggest the quantities of lime needed to counteract any excess. The acidity is expressed by the symbol pH. A soil with a pH of 7 is neutral, soils with a lower reading than this are acid, those with a higher reading are alkaline. The acidity and alkalinity increase as the readings get further away from the neutral mark.

Some caution is needed when it comes to applying the lime as an over-limed soil is as bad as an under-limed one, so do make the test first. I find that a dressing of 75 g per square metre (3 oz per square yard) of hydrated lime is an average application, but on light soils I prefer to use ground limestone because it is not so easily washed out; this should be applied at double the above rate.

Drainage

I have already mentioned the fact that vegetables need moisture-retentive yet well-drained soil. This is not a contradiction in terms, it simply means that the soil should have a sponge-like consistency which will hold a quantity of water while at the same time allowing any excess to drain away. It is in building up this sponge-like character that organic matter is important.

The problem of waterlogging arises when the water table is high or the layer of subsoil immediately under the topsoil is impervious. This means that in periods of heavy rain the water, which cannot drain away quickly enough, collects on top of the subsoil and the topsoil eventually becomes waterlogged.

Drainage problems of this kind need fairly drastic remedies involving the digging of ditches and the laying of drain pipes. This is major construction work and I advise you to seek expert advice and help with it, otherwise you may be put to a lot of work without achieving the results you want.

Seed sowing

The majority of vegetables are grown from seed sown either out of doors or in pots or boxes under glass.

Sowing out of doors

The first outdoor sowings of the year should not be made until the soil temperature starts to rise, so do not be tempted to sow in those deceptively mild periods which sometimes occur in February. I am always guided by the hedges – once these start to show green then this is a good indication that the soil temperature will be right for the first sowings. In general this is likely to be around early March in the South of Britain, late March in the Midlands and early April in the North. The type of soil will also affect the sowing time as light soils warm up much more quickly than heavy clay ones. If you do want to get ahead with the spring sowing, and I think this is a good idea, then the soil should be covered with cloches a few weeks in advance of your intended sowing date. The method of sowing seeds out of doors is shown in the drawings.

Sowing under glass

The vegetables usually sown under glass are early cauliflower, cabbage, Brussels sprouts, onions, leeks, celery, celeriac, marrows, cucumbers, tomatoes, aubergines and peppers. Generally I use seedboxes for these sowings but cucumbers, marrows and melons are often sown in peat pots or small clay or plastic pots from which they can be planted out without any disturbance to the roots.

When it comes to composts for sowing I'm old fashioned enough to use the John Innes seed compost, and the John Innes potting composts for pricking out and potting on. These composts are standardized mixtures of soil, peat and sand with added fertilizers. Although they can be prepared at home it is easier to buy them ready mixed, but they do vary with regard to the quality of the soil used in them.

As a guide I use John Innes potting compost No. 1 for pricking out and the first potting. Then, if the

Good planning means that maximum use is made of the area available

plants are to be grown on in pots, I pot them on progressively into the No. 2 and No. 3 mixtures. The difference in number indicates an increased fertilizer content.

The peat-based composts are good, but they need

Seed sowing under glass Fill the box with compost, firming it well along the edges and in the corners

Give a final firming and smooth the surface with a presser made from a flat piece of wood with a handle

Get the compost moist by holding the seedbox in a container of water until the moisture comes through to the surface

Scatter the seeds thinly over the surface, or place them individually if they are large enough

Sieve a thin layer of compost over the top of the seeds. Label the box with details of the crop sown and the date

Cover the box with a pane of glass and a sheet of paper until germination has occurred

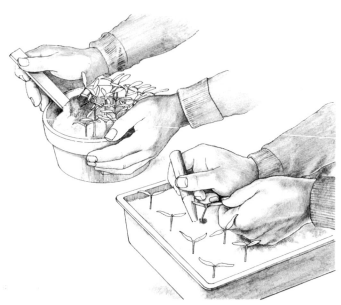

Pricking out Once the seedlings have produced their first leaves loosen the roots (left) and, holding them only by the leaves, transfer them to another container

more careful watering and they tend to produce a more lush plant. However, I think we will eventually have to go over to these because of the shortage of good soil for the John Innes.

Pricking out

As soon as the seedlings are large enough to handle they should be transferred to another container, either a box or pots, where they will have room to grow. This procedure is known as pricking out and it is illustrated in the accompanying drawings.

Hardening off

When the seedlings have established themselves and started to grow they will need to be hardened off. This is a process of acclimatization which enables them to be planted out of doors without any undue set-back. It is done by putting the pots or boxes of young seedlings in a frame and slowly increasing the amount of ventilation by gradually raising the lights, until after several weeks the lights can be removed altogether.

Planting out

Young plants can be planted out using either a trowel or a dibber (see page 32). Mark the row with a line and make the holes large enough to hold the roots comfortably. Firm the plants in well and water them thoroughly.

General cultivation

Frequent hoeing, occasional feeding and watering when necessary are all the aftercare that most vegetables need to make good growth. I use the Dutch hoe more among the vegetables than anywhere else in the garden. This useful tool not only keeps down competing weeds but also stirs up the soil, letting in air and forming a loose dust mulch which helps to prevent loss of moisture from lower down.

An adequate supply of water is necessary if the vegetables are to grow well and give satisfactory yields. Much can be done to improve the water-holding capacity of the soil by digging in organic matter but unless the growing season is wet additional applications of water will be needed. These can be given from a sprinkler system, watering can or through lay-flat polythene tubing. Whichever method is used it is important that watering is done with care, ideally as a gentle slow spray which has the effect of soaking the soil without causing compaction and damage to the soil structure.

In prolonged periods of dry weather there may be a shortage of mains water and if this is the case you may have to establish an order of priority for any water that is available. As far as the vegetables are concerned this priority should be, I think, runner beans, celery, lettuce, newly planted brassica crops, peas and onions.

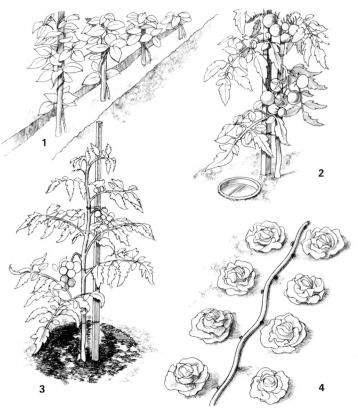

Ways to make watering more effective 1. Plant peas and beans in a trench. **2.** Sink a pot by each tomato plant and water through this. **3.** Mulch plants. **4.** Use irrigation tubing

Pests and diseases

Vegetables are subject to attack from a wide range of pests and diseases. The most prevalent of these, together with suggested control measures, are listed on pages 70 to 73. It is worth noting, however, that well-grown vegetables are less likely to fall prey to attack.

Sowing and Harvesting Chart

	Jan.	Feb.	March	April	May	June	July	Aug.	Sept.	Oct.	Nov.	Dec.
Broad beans	●●	●●●●	●●●●	●●●●	●●●●	●●●●	●	●●●●	●●●●	●●	●●●●	
French beans		●●	●●●		●●●● ●●	●●●●	●●●	●●●●	●●●●	●●●●	●	
Runner beans				●●●	●●●● ●●	●●	●●●	●●●	●●●	●		
Beetroot			●●	●●●●	●●●●	●●●●	●	●●●●	●●●●	●●●●		
Leaf beet	●●●●	●●●●	●●●●	●●●●		●●●	●●●	●●●●	●●●●	●●●●	●●●●	●●●●
Broccoli	●●●●	●●●●	●●●● ●	●●●●	●	●●●	●●●●		●●●●	●●●●	●●●●	●●●●
Brussels sprouts	●●●●	●●●●	●●●● ●	●●●●	●●●	●●●	●●●		●●●●	●●●●	●●●●	●●●●
Cabbage summer	●●●	●●●●	●●●●	●●●●	●●●	●●●	●●●●	●●●●	●●●			
autumn and winter	●●●●	●●●●	●●●	●●	●●●●	●●●●	●●●●			●●●●	●●●●	●●●●
spring		●●●●	●●●●	●●●●	●●●●	●	●●●●	●●●●	●●●●	●●●		
Carrots			●●●●	●●●●	●●●●	●●●●	●●	●●●●	●●●●	●●●●	●	
Cauliflower summer	●●●●	●●●●		●●●●				●●	●●●●	●●●●		
autumn and winter	●●●●	●●●●	●●●●	●●●●	● ●●●●	●●●●	●●●●					
Celery	●●●●		●●●●	●●●●	●	●●●●			●●●●	●●●●	●●●●	●●●●
Cucumber frame			●●●●	●●●●			●●●●	●●●●	●●●●			
ridge				●●●	●●●●		●	●●●●	●●●●	●		
Endive	●●●●	●●●●	●●●●	●●●●	●●●●	●●●●	●●●●	●●●●	●●●●	●●●●	●●●●	●●●●
Kale	●●●●	●●●●	●●●●	●●●●	●●●●		●●●●	●●●●			●●●●	●●●●
Kohl-rabi				●●●●	●●●●	●●●●	●●●	●●●●	●●●●	●●●●	●●●	
Leeks	●●●●	●●●●	●●●●	●●●●	●●●●	●●●●			●●●●	●●●●	●●●●	●●●●
Lettuce	●●●●	●●●●	●●●●	●●●●	●●●●	●●●●	●●●●	●●●●	●●●●	●●●	●●●●	●●●●
Marrow				●●●	●●●●			●●●	●●●●	●●●●		
Onions	●●●●	●	●●●● ●●●●	●●●●	●			●●●●	●●●●	●●●●	●●	●●
Parsnips	●●●●	●●●●	●●●● ●	●●●●	●●●●				●●●●	●●●●	●●●●	●●●●
Peas	●	●●●	●●●●	●●●●	●●●●	●●●	●●●	●●●●	●●●●	●●●●	●● ●●●●	
Peppers			●●●●			●●		●●●●	●●●			
Potatoes early			●●●		●●	●●●●	●●●●					
main crop				●●●				●●	●●●●	●●●		
Radish			●●●	●●●●	●●●● ●●	●●●●	●●●●	●●	●●●●	●●●		
Spinach	●●●●	●●●●	●●●●	●●●●	●●●●	●●●●	●●●●	●●●●	●●●●	●●		●●●●
Swede	●●●●	●●●●	●●		●●●	●●●●				●●●●	●●●●	●●●●
Sweet corn				●●●●	●●●● ●	●			●●●	●●●	●●●	
Tomatoes	●	●	●●●●	●	●	●●		●●●	●●●●	●●		
Turnip	●●●●	●●	●●●● ●	●●●●	●●●●	●●●●	●●●●	●●●●	●	●●●	●●●●	●●●●

●● sowing under glass   ●● sowing out of doors   ●● planting   ●● main harvesting period

Globe Artichoke

Sow: March under glass
April out of doors

Plant: Offsets in early April

Harvest: Late summer, from the second year onwards

Apart from providing us with an excellent vegetable in the form of its tasty flower heads, the globe artichoke is also a very handsome garden plant equally at home in the herbaceous border.
Selected varieties. Green Globe, Green Ball, Large Round French Green.

Globe artichokes should be cut when the heads are plump but before the purple florets show

Soil preparation

A rich, well-dug soil and a sunny position are essential for artichokes. Dig in a good application of manure in the autumn and give a dressing of general fertilizer at the rate of 55 g per square metre (2 oz per square yard) before planting.

Planting

Although globe artichokes can be raised from seed a much more reliable method of propagation is by taking offsets from plants which are known to be good croppers.

Include a small piece of stem

These offsets should be planted 1 m (3 ft) apart in the row and 1 m (3 ft) should also be allowed between each row.

Cultivation

Topdress the plants with compost or manure in May. Remove all the flower spikes in the first year so that the plant concentrates its energy on producing a good sturdy crown.

Cut away the dead outer leaves in autumn and cover the crown with straw, bracken or ashes. The protective material can be removed the following April and the soil around each plant given a dressing of a nitrogenous fertilizer such as sulphate of ammonia at the rate of 55 g per square metre (2 oz per square yard). An occasional application of a general fertilizer should be given through the growing season – two or three applications should be sufficient.

Lift and divide the plants every 3 to 4 years.

Harvesting

The flower heads should be picked as soon as they are plump but before the purple florets show at the top; cut them off with an inch or so of stem. The heads are boiled in water and the fleshy bases of the scales together with the inner base of the flower are eaten, the centre of the flower, which is known as the choke, being thrown away.

Pests and diseases

Blackfly and greenfly may prove a nuisance and slugs may damage both the leaves and the flower heads. See page 70.

Quick tip

If space is limited why not try one or two plants in the flower border?

Jerusalem Artichoke

Jerusalem artichokes are planted in drills which have been taken out with a hoe or spade

Plant: February

Harvest: The following autumn and winter

The tuberous roots of the Jerusalem artichoke have a distinctive and subtle flavour. As well as being eaten like potatoes, they make an unusual and welcome addition to soups and stews.

Selected varieties. The Jerusalem artichoke is a straight species of plant which does not have the usual range of varieties. All plants sold as Jerusalem artichokes will be the same.

Soil preparation

Ordinary soil is quite capable of producing good tubers, but better results will be obtained if the soil is given a good application of compost or manure in the autumn before planting. An open position suits them best although they will grow in partial shade.

Planting

The tubers of the Jerusalem artichoke are rather like very knobbly potatoes and they are planted in the prepared soil 13 cm (5 in) deep and 38 cm (15 in) apart, leaving 75 cm (2½ ft) between the rows.

Cultivation

Little in the way of cultivation is necessary for this easily pleased vegetable. Hoe between the rows occasionally and draw some soil towards the bases of the plants to prevent the tubers being exposed. The stems will grow quite tall – up to 3 m (10 ft) – and may need staking if they occupy an exposed position. In late October cut off the top growth completely.

Harvesting

The tubers are lifted as required from November onwards. Alternatively they can all be lifted at once and stored in the same way as potatoes. Save some of the tubers – preferably medium-sized ones which are of good shape – for planting the following year.

Storing. The tubers can be stored in sand but they tend to lose their flavour.

Pests and Diseases

Slugs may attack the tubers, see page 70.

Quick tip

Jerusalem artichoke plants grow up to 3 m (10 ft) in height and make an excellent temporary screen for the compost heap.

Start to lift the tubers in November and save some for planting the following year

Asparagus

Sow: Early April

Plant: April

Harvest: Spring and early summer, from the third year after planting

This luxury crop is not all that expensive to grow although it is demanding of space and requires a great deal of patience as it is slow to come into cropping.

Selected strains. Regal, Martha Washington, Connover's Colossal.

Soil preparation

Good drainage is essential and as this is a very long-term crop the soil must be properly prepared by digging it deeply and getting rid of all perennial weeds, and then incorporating well-rotted manure or garden compost together with a dressing of bonemeal. Before planting apply lime or ground chalk at 55 g per square metre (2 oz per square yard).

Seed sowing

In a separate seedbed sow thinly in 2·5-cm (1-in) deep drills. Keep weeded and watered and thin the seedlings to 30 cm (12 in). The young plants will be ready for planting out the following April.

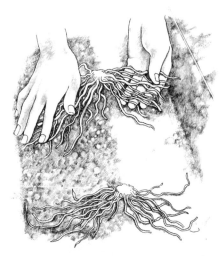

When planting asparagus crowns spread the roots over a low mound of soil

Planting

Use either plants raised from seed or purchased crowns, and I prefer one-year-old crowns as these get away more quickly. For each row take out a trench 15 to 23 cm (6 to 9 in) deep and make a low mound of soil down the centre. Set the crowns 38 cm (15 in) apart on this mound with the roots spread either side. Keep the unplanted crowns covered with damp sacking and cover each crown with soil immediately it is placed in position. Water well after planting. The rows will need to be about 60 cm (2 ft) apart.

Cultivation

First year. Do not cut any of the shoots, the fern should be allowed to grow to build up strong plants. Weed and feed with general fertilizer in the summer and water in dry weather. Cut down the top growth when it changes colour in late autumn and dress the rows with compost or manure.

Earth up the plants in early spring by drawing soil from between the rows to form ridges. Feed in late February with a general fertilizer and every second year with agricultural salt at 55 g per square metre (2 oz per square yard).

Second year. Repeat cultivation requirements of the first year. Level out the ridges in July and push in some pea sticks to support the fern. Do not cut any shoots.

Third and subsequent years. The shoots can be harvested from the third year but do not continue cutting after the third week in June as the fern must be allowed to grow to build up the plants for the following year's crop. Feed with a general fertilizer when cutting is finished. Cut down the fern in late autumn and proceed as in previous years.

Harvesting

Using a sharp, serrated knife, preferably a special asparagus one, cut about 8 cm (3 in) below soil

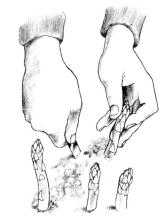

Asparagus is ready for cutting when the shoots are about 10 cm (4 in) above the level of the soil

level when the shoots are showing about 10 cm (4 in). Take care not to damage the crowns or the other developing shoots.

Pests and diseases

Earwigs, slugs and the asparagus beetle may be troublesome, see page 70.

Asparagus is always expensive and is well worth growing if sufficient space is available in the garden

22

Aubergine

Sow: January and February under glass

Plant: Late May

Harvest: August to September

This vegetable, which is also known as the egg plant, is not all that easy to grow but is worth trying if you are looking for something unusual.

Selected varieties. A succulent and readily available variety is Long Purple.

Soil preparation

Though they are only half-hardy plants, aubergines can be planted outside through the summer months in many parts of the country. The soil should be well drained and fertile – a spring dressing of a general fertilizer at the rate of 55 g per square metre (2 oz per square yard) will be helpful – and the site should be as sunny and sheltered as possible.

Seed sowing

The seeds must be sown under glass in January or February in a temperature of 16°C (60°F). Prick out the seedlings into boxes as soon as they are large enough to be handled easily, and when they are about 5 to 8 cm (2 to 3 in) high, pot them into 9-cm (3½-in) pots. If you intend planting the aubergines out-side, now is the time to start hardening off the plants to get them accustomed to the lower tempera-tures.

If the plants are to be cropped in the greenhouse, grow them in slightly warmer temperatures, eventually potting them on into 15- to 18-cm (6- to 7-in) pots in John Innes potting compost No. 3.

Planting

Set out the plants when all danger of frost is past as you would with

Aubergines are one of the more unusual vegetables but are better when grown under glass. It is important to pick the fruits before they lose their shine

outdoor tomatoes. A spacing of 60 cm (2 ft) between plants and rows is adequate. Give each plant a stout 1-m (3-ft) cane.

Cultivation

Pinch out the growing tips when the plants are 15 cm (6 in) high and, when six fruits have set on a plant, stop all the side shoots and remove any further flowers which form. Spraying with water at midday will help the fruits to set.

Outdoor plants will need to be kept weed free and both outdoor and indoor plants should be watered freely and given a liquid feed two or three times during the season.

Harvesting

Fruits should be picked when they are of a usable size but before they lose their shine; as they age they become tough and bitter. Handle the fruits carefully – rather like beetroot they bruise very easily – and eat them as soon as possible after harvesting.

Pests and diseases

Red spider mite and whitefly may be a problem under glass, see page 70.

Quick tip

Aubergines do particularly well when grown in peat bags either in the greenhouse or out of doors. Allow two plants to each bag.

Broad Beans

Sow: November (except in very exposed areas)
Mid-January to February under glass
Mid-February to early July out of doors

Harvest: June to October

This crop is grown for the large beans within the pods.

Selected varieties. Aquadulce is a useful kind which I use for the November sowing or as the first sowing under glass. For later sowings Colossal, Masterpiece, Green Longpod, Imperial White Windsor are recommended. The Sutton, a dwarf kind, is good as a maincrop as well as being useful for sowing as a catch crop in July to give beans for picking in October.

The broad bean Green Windsor is another good variety which is useful for freezing

Soil preparation

Broad beans need a soil containing a good supply of well-rotted garden compost or manure. I apply a dressing of general fertilizer before sowing and one of hydrated lime after digging if the soil is acid.

Seed sowing

Sow the seeds 5 cm (2 in) deep and 15 cm (6 in) apart in double rows 23 cm (9 in) apart. Successive pairs of rows should be 1 m (3 ft) apart. Sown in this way the plants will help to support each other and will need little additional support other than strings carried down the outsides of the rows and attached to posts at either end.

The November sowing is more likely to be successful in areas where the winters are mild. However, if a greenhouse or frame is available then early sowings can be made, the seeds being placed either singly in small pots or spaced 5 to 8 cm (2 to 3 in) apart in boxes. Young plants should be hardened off and

Broad beans can be sown out of doors in drills or in boxes or pots under glass

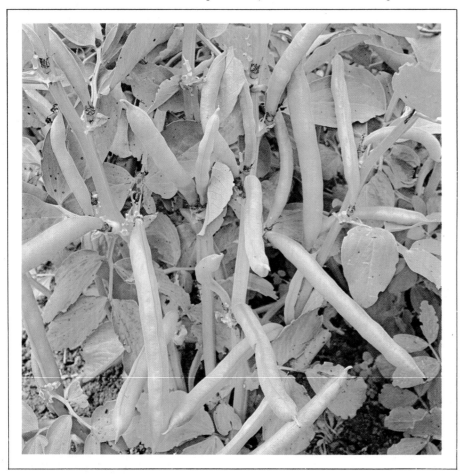

planted out in April, with cloche protection if the weather is cold.

Cultivation

Hoe regularly, removing any suckers which form around the bases of the plants, and water well in dry weather. When the clusters of beans begin to set spray with a systemic insecticide to discourage attacks of blackfly and pinch out the tips of the shoots.

Harvesting

It is important to pick when the pods are well filled and before the beans become tough and mealy. Test a sample pod at intervals – the beans have passed their best when they have developed black eyes.

Pests and diseases

Blackfly is a certain pest and chocolate spot the most likely disease. See pages 70 to 73.

French Beans

Sow: January to February under glass for indoor cropping
Mid-April under glass
Late April to June out of doors

Harvest: May and June under glass
July to October out of doors

There are two kinds of French beans, the dwarf and the climbing, but it is the first which I think are of the greatest value to the gardener.

Selected varieties. The Prince and Sprite crop and freeze well, other good varieties include Masterpiece, Canadian Wonder, Tendergreen, Earligreen (all dwarf kinds), and Blue Lake White Seeded and Earliest of All (climbing kinds).

French beans should be picked regularly or they will stop cropping. The beans are ready when they reach a usable size and can be snapped cleanly

Soil preparation

The soil should be limed if it is acid, well dug, manured, and dressed with a general fertilizer before sowing.

Seed sowing

Sow the seeds thinly in drills 2·5 cm (1 in) deep and spaced 45 to 60 cm (18 to 24 in) apart for dwarf kinds and 1 m (3 ft) for climbing varieties. Thin the seedlings to 15 to 23 cm (6 to 9 in) apart.

French beans, almost more than any other crop, require a warm soil, so it is important not to sow them too early – cloches can be used to boost the soil temperature prior to sowing and with cloche protection sowing in late April is possible. Under glass the seeds can be sown in peat pots in mid-April for planting outside in early June.

I find it very useful to have an early crop of beans grown under glass. For this I use The Prince and sow in January or February placing the seeds either singly in peat pots or 5 to a 13-cm (5-in) pot. These are repotted into 18-cm (7-in) pots. From 20 such pots we get several good pickings in late May and through June.

Pot-grown beans provide an early crop

A sowing out of doors in late June provides beans for picking in late September or early October. And a later autumn crop can be obtained by sowing in July in frames or giving cloche protection to the rows.

Cultivation

Hoe and water well in dry weather. Spray the plants with water to help the flowers to set.

Climbing varieties will need to be supported – bean poles, bamboo canes or netting can be used – and the dwarf kinds are usually better for having some soil drawn up around their stems.

Harvesting

Pick regularly once the beans reach a usable size and can be snapped cleanly.

Pests and diseases

Blackfly and red spider mites are the pests to look out for. See page 70.

Runner Beans

Sow: April to May under glass
May to June out of doors

Harvest: July to October

This is my favourite vegetable and a most worthwhile crop to grow as it gives an exceptionally high yield.

Selected varieties. Streamline and Scarlet Emperor grow well for me. White-flowered varieties are thought by some people to perform better in hot, dry summers, and White Achievement is a good one. Another variety much recommended for its flavour and heavy crops is the pink-flowered Sunset.

Soil preparation

For a heavy crop of runner beans it is essential that the soil has been well prepared and contains a good supply of organic matter in the

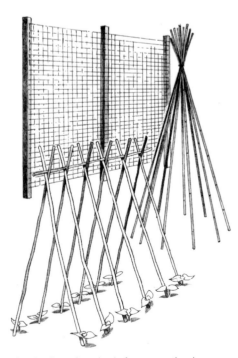

A selection of methods for supporting beans. Make sure that the one chosen is secure

form of manure or compost. Before sowing add some general fertilizer. If the soil is acid apply a dressing of ground chalk or hydrated lime during the winter.

Seed sowing

This is a very tender crop and care is needed with the sowing times – late April is the earliest possible date for sowing outside in warm areas and, generally, I think it is safer to wait until mid-May and to give cloche protection.

Sow the seeds 5 cm (2 in) deep and 23 to 30 cm (9 to 12 in) apart in a double row 30 cm (12 in) apart. For most families one such double row 4 or more metres (13 or more feet) long should provide a sufficient crop but if more are required then successive double rows must be spaced 1·5 m (5 ft) apart.

To get well ahead with the crop I like to sow singly in 8-cm (3-in) pots or peat pots at the end of April and to plant out at the end of May or early June depending on the frost situation in the district.

Cultivation

One supporting cane should be provided for each plant – a loop of string placed around the young shoot and the cane will encourage the growth in the right direction. As runner beans are a heavy crop when fully grown the supporting canes must be securely fixed to each other by crossing the tops and tying them to another cane to form a continuous structure. Other means of support can be employed, such as wigwams of canes or the special netting available for this purpose. All types of support need to be firm and securely anchored.

When the plants reach the tops of the poles the tip of each should be pinched out to encourage the formation of side shoots.

Water freely throughout the season and spray the plants with water to set the flowers. Dryness at the roots is often a cause of beans failing to set and if possible a mulch of some form of organic matter applied in June will help with water

Runner beans are one of the most useful of vegetable crops but they do need a sunny site and plenty of moisture

retention. Feed during August with liquid fertilizer.

It is possible to grow runner beans without support by continually pinching out the growing points and allowing the plants to trail over the ground. The beans will be somewhat crooked but the flavour is the same.

Harvesting

Start picking as soon as the beans reach a usable size, and can be snapped cleanly. Pick regularly, making sure that no beans are left to mature as once this happens the setting of new beans will cease.

Pests and diseases

Blackfly is likely to be the most troublesome, see page 70.

Other troubles. Failure of the flowers to set may be caused by cold nights or dry soil or a combination of the two. Watering and thorough preparation of the soil are, therefore, very important.

Beetroot

Sow: March to July

Harvest: July to October

There are three main types of beetroot which are sown to give a succession of roots and each particular type has many varieties.
Selected varieties. The globe-rooted types are best for early sowings and of these I recommend Crimson Globe and Sutton's Globe as being particularly good, and also Boltardy which, as its name suggests, is not as prone to bolting as some of the early sown kinds. Tankard and long-rooted kinds should be sown for mid-season and late crops and I find Cheltenham Greentop and Housewives' Choice ideal.

After lifting beetroot cut or twist off the foliage but take care not to damage the flesh

Soil preparation

Beetroot needs a deeply cultivated soil and preferably one which has been manured for a previous crop – freshly manured soil will produce forked and distorted roots. Before sowing, I always dust the soil with a general fertilizer at the rate of 55 to 110 g per square metre (2 to 4 oz per square yard).

Seed sowing

Using the variety Boltardy, a first sowing can be made in mid-March, but with other varieties sowings made much before mid-April are likely to bolt or fail completely due to the cold and wet conditions which are often prevalent at this time of the year.

Sow the tankard and long-rooted kinds from May onwards. The seed should be sown in drills 2·5 cm (1 in) deep and 38 cm (15 in) apart. Do not sow in a continuous line but group two or three seeds every 15 to 20 cm (6 to 8 in); this makes thinning easier. I like to thin the seedlings when they are about 5 cm (2 in) high leaving one from each group.

Cultivation

Hoe between the rows regularly and hand weed between the individual plants when necessary. Take care that the seedlings are not allowed to dry out in hot weather.

Harvesting

Lift the roots when they are about the size of a tennis ball, removing the leaves by twisting or cutting them off as near to the crown as possible but taking care not to damage the flesh.

Storing. I always store some of the later-maturing crops in boxes of light soil or sand in a frostproof shed; in this way the season of use can be extended. Take particular care that the roots selected for storing are not damaged – bruised roots will quickly rot.

Pests and diseases

Damping off may occur in early sowings if conditions are cold and damp. The main pest likely to cause trouble is blackfly. See pages 70 to 73.

Other troubles. On very stony or freshly manured ground the roots may become forked and distorted and if heavy autumn rains follow a summer dry spell the roots may split.

Quick tip

For a change of colour and flavour why not use the Golden Beet to add variety to summer salads.

27

Leaf Beet

Sow: April to July

Harvest: July to March

Under this general heading can be found the various forms of beet which are grown for their spinach-like leaves. They are especially useful as they are hardy and crop for months longer than spinach. The three main types are Perpetual Spinach, Ruby or Rhubarb Chard and Silver or Seakale Beet. The last is also known as Swiss Chard. Ruby Chard is very ornamental in the flower garden.

Soil preparation

This is the same as for beetroot but as the roots are not cropped it does not matter if the soil has been freshly manured.

Seed sowing

Sow in succession from April to July to maintain a year-round supply. The drills should be 2·5 cm (1 in) deep and 45 cm (18 in) apart. Thin the plants to 23 cm (9 in).

Cultivation

Keep the hoe going regularly and water in dry weather. If the soil is on the poor side then dress with a high nitrogen fertilizer at 55 g per square metre (2 oz per square yard).

Harvesting

Pick in the same way as spinach, pulling the leaves as required from the outside of each plant. It is important to pick and eat them while they are young. The chards have an added value as the thick midribs can be stripped from the leaves and cooked separately – they have a taste resembling that of seakale.

Pests and diseases

Birds and slugs are likely to do the most damage but these should not be unduly troublesome. See page 70.

The colourful Rhubarb Chard is a dual-purpose vegetable as the leaves and midribs can be eaten separately

Broccoli

Sow: March to May

Plant: June and July

Harvest: September to June

Sprouting broccoli is a most useful long-term winter and spring vegetable. Heading broccoli is now included under cauliflower.

Selected varieties. Calabrese will be ready from September; the large central head should be cut first and this is then followed by numerous side shoots. White and Purple Sprouting carry the cropping season well on into the New Year.

Soil preparation

Soil which has been manured for a previous crop is the best and I always make sure that it has been well firmed, and dressed with lime if it is acid.

Seed sowing

The seed should be sown in a separate seedbed which has been well firmed and raked to give a good tilth. No manure is necessary but a dressing of lime at 110 g per square metre (4 oz per square

The central head of this calabrese-type broccoli is ready for harvesting

yard) is helpful. Sow in 1-cm (½-in) deep drills spaced 23 cm (9 in) apart and I like to dust each drill with calomel dust before sowing to ward off club root and flea beetle.

Planting

This is done when the seedlings are about 5 cm (2 in) high. Water the seedbed the day before lifting. Discard any plants which lack a growing point or have bent stems and dip the roots of the remainder into a paste made from calomel dust and water. I use a dibber to make the planting holes and in dry weather I fill each hole with water and allow this to drain away before setting the plant into position. It should go in as far as the lowest leaves and be well firmed. Set the plants 60 cm (2 ft) apart with 1 m (3 ft) between rows.

Cultivation

Hoe regularly. Feed once or twice with a general fertilizer before the flower buds start to form. In the autumn draw some soil up around the stems to improve the anchorage.

Harvesting

Pick as soon as the flower shoots are well formed but before the flowers open; include 13 to 15 cm (5 to 6 in) of stem.

Pests and diseases

Broccoli is one of the brassica crops and is affected by the same pests and diseases as cabbage, see page 32.

Quick tip

To succeed with both broccoli and cauliflower the plants must be kept growing. Watch that the young plants are not given a check through being starved by leaving them too long in pots, boxes or the seedbox.

Cut the side shoots of sprouting broccoli with several inches of stem

Brussels Sprouts

Sow: February under glass or in a frame
March to April out of doors

Plant: April, May, June

Harvest: September to early spring

This crop is a good winter standby and I favour sowing in April so that picking need not start before the main autumn vegetables have come to an end.

Selected varieties. Peer Gynt and Citadel both freeze well for me and Market Rearguard is a useful late-maturing kind. I do like the F_1 varieties for their compactness and uniformity of cropping.

Soil preparation

A good rich soil manured for a previous crop is ideal. It must be well firmed and dressed with lime if it is at all acid.

Seed sowing

Under glass sow thinly in boxes. Out of doors sow in a seedbed of well-firmed soil which has been raked to a fine tilth. The drills should be 1 cm ($\frac{1}{2}$ in) deep and 23 cm (9 in) apart.

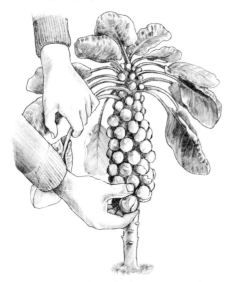

Pick the sprouts from the bottom upwards

A well-grown plant should produce a good crop of firm sprouts. The tops can also be eaten after the sprouts have been harvested

Planting

From sowings made under glass young plants can be set out in April; from outdoor sowings in May and June. Water the seedbed well the day before planting. Set the plants 1 m (3 ft) apart in each direction making the planting holes with a dibber. If the ground is at all dry then I fill each hole with water and allow this to drain away before putting the plant in position and firming the soil well around it.

Cultivation

Water well in dry weather and keep the hoe going. Feed occasionally with a high nitrogen fertilizer at 25 g to the metre run (1 oz to the yard run) but not after mid-August.

In the autumn draw some earth up around the stems to steady the plants against wind rock. Remove any yellowing leaves.

Harvesting

Pick from the bottom of the stems upwards as soon as the lowermost sprouts are a usable size.

Pests and diseases

This is another of the brassica crops and prone to attack by the same pests and diseases as cabbage, see page 32.

Other troubles. The appearance of loose-leaved blown sprouts usually means that either the soil was inadequately firmed or too much compost or manure has been added. I have found that early sowing in cold soil or dry conditions with insufficient watering has the same effect.

Quick tip

To produce good solid sprouts you need soil which is almost as hard as a road. Dig it over before planting and then tread really well.

Cabbage

Summer cabbage
Early
Sow: January to February under glass
Plant: March to April
Harvest: May and June
Maincrop
Sow: Early March to late April
Plant: April to June
Harvest: July to September

Autumn cabbage
Sow: Late April
Plant: Early June
Harvest: October

Winter cabbage
Sow: Throughout May
Plant: June, July
Harvest: November to January

Savoys
Sow: April to May
Plant: July to August
Harvest: October to March

Spring cabbage
Sow: July to August
Plant: September to October
Harvest: Spring

Cabbage provides us with crops all the year round although it will be necessary to grow a range of varieties to achieve this.

Selected varieties. The spring sowings under glass begin, with me, with varieties such as May Star and June Star, and Hispi is another one well worth a try. Then come Greyhound and Winnigstadt, both sown out of doors, and a red cabbage – Large Blood Red – for pickling.

Market Topper and Autumn Supreme are useful autumn-heading kinds, and for my money January King is one of the best of the winter cabbages. Winter White and Christmas Drumhead are also good at this time as well as the savoys Ormskirk Late and Rearguard.

For spring cropping there are Harbinger, Offenham, Wheeler's Imperial, Evesham and April.

Soil preparation

A rich, well-firmed soil manured for a previous crop is required. If the soil is acid apply lime at 85 g to the square metre (3 oz to the square yard) and I like to add a dressing of general fertilizer at 55 g to the square metre (2 oz to the square yard) before planting.

Seed sowing

Sow the different kinds of cabbage at the times indicated above in a well-firmed seedbed in drills 1 cm ($\frac{1}{2}$ in) deep and 23 cm (9 in) apart.

The first sowing of summer-heading cabbages is made in boxes or peat pots in a cool greenhouse or frame.

Planting

Water the seedbed the day before lifting. Inspect the plants and discard any with bent stems or without growing points. With the exception of the spring cabbages all are set out 45 cm (18 in) apart in rows 60 cm (2 ft) apart. The spring cabbage are spaced 30 cm (12 in) apart in rows 45 cm (18 in) apart.

Quick tip

Chinese cabbage is an interesting variation which is equally good cooked or eaten raw. Sow the seeds where they are to mature in July and thin to 30 cm (12 in). Sampan, Nagaoka and Pe-tsai seem to me rather appropriately named varieties.

I mark the position of the row with a line and then use a dibber to make the planting holes. When the soil is dry I find it helpful to fill each hole with water and allow this to drain away before setting the plants down to their lowest leaves and planting them firmly.

Cultivation

Cabbages withstand drought better than most of the brassicas but they do need regular hoeing to keep them weed free.

January King is one of the best of the winter cabbages. It is ready for use in January

Fine specimens of the spring-heading cabbage Evesham

I feed the summer, autumn and winter cabbage once in summer with a nitrogenous fertilizer, such as Nitro-chalk, at 55 g to the square metre (2 oz to the square yard). The spring cabbage should not be fed until all the frosts are over.

During the winter make routine checks of the plants and firm in any that have been lifted by the frost.

Harvesting

When the hearts are solid lift the plants with a fork and cut off the stalk, roots and outer leaves. Spring cabbages may be pulled before they have hearted up and eaten as spring greens.

Pests and diseases

Cabbages, together with broccoli, brussels sprouts, cauliflower, kale, kohl-rabi, swedes, and turnips, make up a group of vegetables collectively known as brassicas. This group, more than any of the other vegetable crops, is especially susceptible to a range of pests and one particularly important disease.

The insect pests to watch for are aphids, cabbage root fly, flea beetle, whitefly, and the caterpillars of the cabbage white butterfly and cabbage moth, all of which can be controlled by chemical means.

Pigeons are especially fond of young brassica plants and are, on the whole, more difficult to control. I have found that the only sure way of deterring them is by draping the rows with netting.

The fungal disease is club root, and very difficult it is to get rid of once the soil is infected. Swollen nodules on the roots followed by decay are typical symptoms. The more acid the soil, the more likely it is that the fungus will get a hold, so unless your soil is alkaline apply a dressing of ground chalk or hydrated lime before planting. It is also advisable to follow some system of crop rotation so that brassicas are not grown on the same site two years running. Club root infection may arrive in the garden on the roots of young plants bought in, or even in farmyard manure if the animals which provide the litter have been fed on infected swedes or other brassicas.

See pages 70 to 73 for control measures.

Other troubles. Crops which fail to heart indicate that either there is too little organic matter in the soil or that the soil was not firmed enough at planting time.

Transplanting cabbages Loosen the soil with a fork before lifting the young plants and take care not to damage the roots

Plant with a dibber, setting the young plants down as far as the first leaves and firming them in well

To test that the plants are in firmly enough, pull a leaf to make sure that they will not lift out of the soil

Carrots

Sow: March under cloches
April to July without protection

Harvest: June onwards

Rather like beetroot, carrots are grouped according to the shape of their roots; the main types being stump rooted, intermediate or long rooted.

Selected varieties. For the earliest sowings I use the stump rooted Amstel and Scarlet Horn, following these up with sowings of Chantenay Red Cored and Favourite (stump rooted) and St Valery and Autumn King (long rooted) to give maincrop and late supplies.

The stump-rooted carrot Favourite is a useful maincrop variety

Soil preparation

Well-worked ground is essential for carrots and soils with a light, sandy texture are preferable. A dressing of general fertilizer at the rate of 55 g per square metre (2 oz per square yard) will be beneficial, but compost or manure should not be added

When lifting carrots for storing cut off their foliage and pack them in boxes

as this will only encourage the roots to fork.

Seed sowing

The earliest crops are sown in drills 1 cm ($\frac{1}{2}$ in) deep and 20 cm (8 in) apart and cloches are placed over the rows until early or mid-April. I like to sow sections of a row at fortnightly intervals to give a succession. Maincrop sowings are made at the same depth but the rows are spaced at 30-cm (12-in) intervals.

Thin the seedlings, leaving one every 10 to 20 cm (4 to 8 in), when the roots are beginning to thicken up. The thinnings are very sweet and well worth eating.

Cultivation

Hoe between the rows frequently and keep an eye open for carrot fly damage, often characterized by wilting and reddening of the leaves. Dust the soil with naphthalene to discourage attack.

Harvesting

Lift the roots as soon as they are of a satisfactory size.
Storing. Carrots harvested in

October can be stored in boxes of dry sand in a frostproof shed or garage. Remove the tops as close to the crown as possible.

Pests and diseases

Carrot fly and slugs are the major pests. See page 70.

Other troubles. Forking of the roots indicates that the ground is either too stony or too rich in organic matter. Splitting may occur as a result of heavy rain following a prolonged dry spell.

Quick tip

To discourage attacks of carrot fly, sow the seed very thinly in the drills and then do not thin the young plants. Soil disturbance at thinning time releases the pungent aroma of the carrot which attracts the carrot fly.

Cauliflower

Summer heading

Sow: Late September or January or February under glass

Plant: April

Harvest: June to July

Autumn and winter heading

Sow: Late April to May

Plant: June to July

Harvest: August to June

This is my favourite of the brassicas and one we particularly like for freezing.

Selected varieties. Snowball, Dominant and Alpha are good summer-heading varieties. These may be followed by White Heart, Flora Blanca and the Australian varieties such as Barrier Reef and Canberra, while All The Year Round covers a long period depending on the time of sowing. Snow's Winter White, St George, Walcheren and Late Queen provide a succession for winter to early summer heading.

Soil preparation

Cauliflowers require a good, deeply dug, well-firmed and well-manured soil and a sunny sheltered position. I do not recommend summer cauliflowers for areas with hot summers and dry soil.

Hoe in a general fertilizer (55 g per square metre, 2 oz per square yard) before transplanting.

Seed sowing

Under glass sowings are made in boxes and the young seedlings pricked out into 8-cm (3-in) peat pots and hardened off in frames for planting out of doors in April.

Outside sowings are made in a well-firmed seedbed in 1-cm (½-in) deep drills.

Planting

Water the seedbed the day before transplanting. The summer varieties are set out in their cropping positions 45 cm (18 in) apart in rows 60 cm (2 ft) apart; the winter ones 60 cm (2 ft) by 75 cm (2½ ft). Fill each planting hole with water and allow this to drain away before placing the plant in position and firming it well.

Cultivation

Hoe regularly and water freely in dry weather. Feed with a general fertilizer at 55 g per square metre (2 oz per square yard) if growth is slow.

Check and firm any plants which may have been lifted by frost.

When the curds form, break or tie some of the inner leaves over them to give them protection and keep them white.

Harvesting

Cut with a sharp knife as soon as they are well grown and the separate sections of the curd can be easily seen. Do not leave them standing after this as the curd separates and the vegetable spoils.

Pests and diseases

This is another of the brassica crops and as such is subject to a number of pests and diseases, see under cabbage.

Other troubles. Poor curd production and plants which run up to seed result from the soil not being firm enough.

Heartless crops indicate a lack of organic matter, which in turn results in the soil having a low moisture-holding capacity. It is important that cauliflowers suffer no check to growth as they have a tendency to go blind – do not delay transplanting once the plants can be handled easily.

To produce a cauliflower with a good curd make sure that the soil is well firmed

Celeriac

Sow: March under glass

Plant: Late May, early June

Harvest: September to March

This useful crop, a stump-rooted version of celery, is particularly good in soups and grated for salads.
Selected varieties. Globus, Marble Ball and Alabaster.

Soil preparation

The soil should be well dug and contain manure or well-rotted garden compost and I add a dressing of general fertilizer at 55g per square metre (2 oz per square yard) before sowing.

Seed sowing

The temperature is all-important for good germination so seeds should be sown in a warm greenhouse. Prick out the seedlings when they

To grow good celeriac prepare the soil by digging in manure or well-rotted compost

are about 5 cm (2 in) high into boxes or small pots.

Harden off the plants and plant outside in late May or early June, spacing them 30 cm (12 in) apart in rows 45 cm (18 in) apart. Plant firmly but not too deeply.

Cultivation

As with all vegetables I like to keep the hoe going regularly and as this is a crop with a high moisture requirement I water well in dry weather.

No earthing up is needed but any side growths which appear should be removed.

Harvesting and storing

Celeriac is ready for lifting in the autumn. In milder areas the roots can be left in the ground for the winter, or they can be lifted before the heavy frosts and stored in boxes of sand. In this case it will be necessary to cut off all the leaves except for the tuft in the centre.

Pests and diseases

Celeriac is subject to the same range of pests and diseases as celery, but few of these are likely to be troublesome.

Celeriac is ready for harvesting from the early autumn. Loosen the roots with a fork before lifting them

Celery

Sow: March or April under glass

Plant: Late May, June

Harvest: Late summer to winter

There is a great deal of satisfaction to be gained in growing celery well as it is not the easiest of crops. Three kinds are available: the hardier white, pink and red for autumn and winter harvesting, and the self-blanching for summer and autumn use.

Selected varieties. I think Solid White is one of the best for the period from October to Christmas and Giant Red for its long-standing qualities which will take it well into the New Year. A reliable self-blanching one for use from August is Golden Self-blanching.

Soil preparation

Celery needs quantities of moisture and food so a deeply dug, well-manured soil is essential. Before planting out fork in a general fertilizer at 40 g per metre run (1½ oz per yard run).

Seed sowing

The seeds are small and germination slow so I like to sow them in a warm greenhouse (16°C, 60°F). The seedlings are pricked out into boxes and hardened off for planting out in May and June.

Planting

The white and the pink or red kinds need blanching and the best way of doing this is to dig a trench 45 cm (1½ ft) deep. Mix well-rotted compost with the excavated soil and return this to the trench to leave a final depth of 15 cm (6 in) below the surrounding soil level; the surplus soil is used to build ridges on either side. The plants should be set out 23 to 30 cm (9 to 12 in) apart down the centre of each

Self-blanching celery can be grown without any earthing up

trench. Water in well and space subsequent trenches 1 m (3 ft) apart.

The self-blanching type does not need a trench and instead is planted out in blocks 23 cm (9 in) apart in each direction.

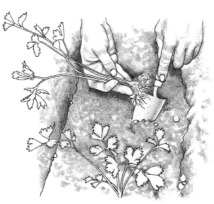

Young celery plants should be set out 23 to 30 cm (9 to 12 in) apart in a trench

Cultivation

Water copiously in dry weather and feed with weak liquid manure or general fertilizer when the plants are established.

Earthing up. When the plants are 25 to 30 cm (10 to 12 in) high start to blanch those varieties which need

it. First remove any offsets and then wrap 8-cm (3-in) deep bands of newspaper around the stems, securing this with string or raffia but allowing room for the hearts to develop. Then, keeping all soil away from the hearts, gradually draw the soil up around the plants. This process is repeated a couple more times as the plants grow until only the top tufts of leaves are showing. During severe weather protect the tops with bracken, straw or peat.

Harvesting

Lift all self-blanching celery before the frosts. The other sorts can remain in the soil and be dug up as required.

Pests and diseases

Celery fly may be troublesome and also celery leaf spot. Brown decay in the centre of the plants indicates soft rot, which may be caused by boron deficiency. See pages 70 to 73.

Other troubles. Plants which receive any sort of check, either through lack of water at any stage or by being left in their seedboxes too long, are liable to run up to seed.

Quick tip

The celery varieties which require blanching do take up a lot of space and I utilize some of this by growing catch crops of lettuce and radish in between.

Chicory

Sow: April to June

Harvest: Throughout the winter months

Although not as frequently grown as it might be, chicory makes a good winter alternative to more conventional salad crops.
   Selected varieties. Witloof.

Soil preparation

A deep, well-cultivated soil which has been manured for a previous crop is just the place for sowing chicory.

Seed sowing

Sow the seed thinly in drills 1 cm ($\frac{1}{2}$ in) deep and 38 cm (15 in) apart, thinning the seedlings when they are 5 cm (2 in) high to leave one every 30 cm (12 in).

Cut the blanched shoots of chicory just above the level of the roots

Cultivation

The aim during the summer is to produce good roots, so any flowers that form on the plants should be removed. Hoe between the plants and water them in dry weather. In November cut the leaves back to about 2·5 cm (1 in) above the crown and lift the roots. These should now be about 30 cm (12 in) long and 8 cm (3 in) across at the top. Trim the roots back to 20 cm (8 in) or so and store them in sand or fine soil in a cool but frostproof shed or garage.

Forcing. The roots are forced a few at a time to give a steady succession. Place them close together and the right way up in large pots or deep boxes, filling in around them with old seed or potting compost or moist peat. As a rough guide, five roots will fit in a 23-cm (9-in) pot. The containers must now be kept in the dark and a good way of doing this is to invert a slightly larger pot over those planted in pots, taking care to cover the hole in the bottom. Roots planted in boxes can be covered with another box or with a deep layer of moist peat or sand. The containers can now be stored in any

Forcing chicory roots under a pot

convenient place, provided that the temperature can be kept in the region of 10 to 13°C (50 to 55°F). The forced and blanched leaves will be ready for cutting and eating in about three weeks.

Harvesting

Remove the shoots (or chicons as they are often called) by cutting them off cleanly just above the crown when they are about 18 cm (7 in) high. The roots will be exhausted after forcing and are best discarded – new ones being raised from seed the following year.

Pests and diseases

Few, if any, troubles are likely to accompany the growing of chicory but watch out for slugs. See page 70.

Quick tip

If indoor facilities are not available for forcing, the plants can be forced and blanched in rows out of doors either by covering the crowns with flower pots or by earthing up as for celery.

Cucumber

Sow:
Frame type March to late April
Ridge type Mid-April under glass
May out of doors

Harvest: July to September

Cucumbers are a crop I enjoy growing, and the secret of growing them successfully is to grow them fast. Cucumbers raised in this way are never bitter.

Of the two main kinds, the ridge is intended for growing out of doors and the frame for cultivation in a greenhouse or garden frame.

Selected varieties. For greenhouse and garden frame – Improved Telegraph, Butcher's Disease Resisting, and the all-female varieties which are becoming increasingly popular, Pepinex, Femdan and Fertila are typical of these.

Ridge kinds include Burpee Hybrid, Gherkin (for pickling), and Apple-shaped with its interesting small fruits. Patio-Pik is a newish variety which crops well.

Ridge cucumbers

Soil preparation. Good soil preparation is all important. Choose a sunny sheltered position and build up a mound or ridge of soil mixed with well-rotted manure or compost.

Seed sowing. Under glass sow the seeds singly, and for this I use peat pots. Harden off and plant out 1 to 1·25 m (3 to 4 ft) apart in the prepared ridge or mound in late May, or early May with cloche protection. If you are sowing out of doors then mid-May is the time; I like to sow groups of 3 seeds 2·5 cm (1 in) deep and 1 m (3 ft) apart, thinning to leave the strongest plant in each position.

Cultivation. When six leaves have formed pinch out the tip of the stem, train the resulting side shoots around the plant and peg them to the soil. Water well and feed weekly with weak liquid manure from the time the first fruits start to swell. White roots appear periodically on the surface and these should be covered with more soil.

As with all the cucumber family –marrows, pumpkins, melons, etc. – two sorts of flowers are produced, male and female. These are readily distinguished by the presence of an immature fruit underneath the female flower in contrast to the male flower which has a slender stem. Ridge cucumbers require the female flower to be pollinated so the male ones must not be removed.

A piece of wood, glass, or slate should be placed under each developing fruit to protect it.

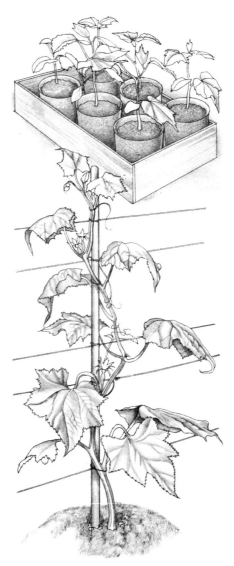

Top Cucumber plants ready for planting out.
Above Set the young plant on a mound of soil and train it upwards

Harvesting. Cut regularly as soon as the cucumbers reach a usable size and when there is still a trace of the flower at the tip.

Frame cucumbers

Seed sowing. Under glass sow singly in peat pots; a temperature of 18°C (65°F) is necessary for germination.

Planting. Make up mounds of well-rotted manure or compost covered with John Innes potting compost No. 3, or one of the peat-based mixtures, on the floor or staging and plant out the seedlings in mid-April or May. When doing this it is important to plant the seedlings on a slight mound to discourage attacks of stem rot.

Train wires along the house at 38-cm (15-in) intervals or position canes to support the growths. Allow the main stems to reach the apex of the roof before removing the growing points. Train the side shoots along the wires, pinching the tips at the second leaf joint.

Spray the plants daily with water to maintain a moist atmosphere but water the soil carefully as it must not be allowed to become waterlogged. At intervals throughout the growing season you will notice fine white roots on the surface of the mounds, these should be covered with 1 cm ($\frac{1}{2}$ in) of compost whenever they appear. In hot weather ventilate the house, preferably from the ridge ventilators, and apply some form of shading to the glass.

Remove all the male flowers as soon as they appear because if the female flowers are pollinated they will produce bitter, bulb-ended fruits. This is unnecessary with the all-female varieties which do not form male flowers. Give a dressing of liquid manure when the first fruits start to develop and continue weekly.

Cultivation in frames

Sow the seeds under glass as already described. Make a mound of John Innes potting compost No. 3 (or peat-based compost) mixed with well-rotted manure or garden

The task of removing the male flowers is unnecessary if an all-female variety of cucumber is grown

compost in the centre of each frame and set one plant on each mound, planting out in April in heated frames but not until the end of May in unheated ones. Pinch out the tip of the plant when six leaves have formed. Four of the side shoots are allowed to develop and are spread evenly to the corners of the frame and pegged to the soil. Each of these shoots should be stopped one leaf beyond the fruit.

Remove the male flowers and grow on as described above. Protect the young fruits by placing a piece of glass or wood underneath each.

When growing cucumbers in frames I pay particular attention to shading the glass as there is a danger of the foliage scorching.

Pests and diseases

Look out for aphids, and whitefly and red spider under glass. Mildew and stem rot are the most likely diseases, although stem rot should not be troublesome if the plants are watered carefully. Symptoms of virus may also be seen and affected plants will need to be destroyed. See pages 70 to 73.

Quick tip

Peat bags provide an easy way of raising cucumbers either out of doors or under glass. Plant two seedlings in each bag and grow on as previously described.

Endive

Sow: April to August

Harvest: August to March

Rather like a cut-leaved lettuce in appearance, the endive is a delicately flavoured salad crop which deserves to be more widely grown.

Selected varieties. Exquisite Curled and Moss Curled are perhaps the most popular varieties, but for later sowings try Winter Lettuce-leaved, with larger, uncut leaves, and Batavian Green.

Soil preparation

Endive is demanding as vegetables go, liking a rich, well-cultivated soil and an open and sunny situation. Light soils are preferable to those with a high clay content. I find that a dressing of super-phosphate of lime applied at the rate of 25 g per square metre (1 oz per square yard) just before planting gives the plants just the start they need.

Seed sowing

Sow thinly in drills 1 cm ($\frac{1}{2}$ in) deep and 30 cm (12 in) apart and thin the seedlings when they are 4 to 5 cm ($1\frac{1}{2}$ to 2 in) high to leave one every 23 cm (9 in). For later sowings the drills should be 38 cm (15 in)

Quick tip

The broad-leaved endive can easily be blanched by tying the leaves together at the top to exclude light from the centre of the plant.

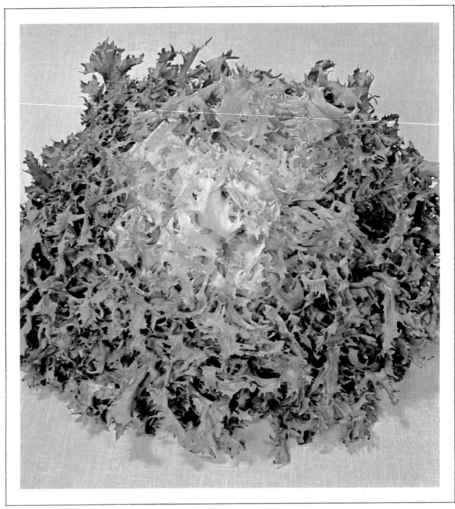

Endive makes a useful alternative to lettuce for winter salads

apart and the seedlings thinned to the same distance.

Cultivation

Endive needs to be grown quickly in summer and may need a top-dressing of nitrate of soda, Nitro-chalk or sulphate of ammonia at 25 g to a 4-metre run (1 oz to 12 ft). Hoe regularly and give plenty of water.

When the plants are well grown, say 23 cm (9 in) across, they will need blanching as this improves the flavour. Wait until the plants are dry and then cover each with an inverted flower pot. As it is important that no light reaches the plants make sure that you have also covered the drainage holes of the pot. Blanching takes about three weeks in summer. To blanch only the hearts of the plants place a saucer over the middle of each one.

The later sown crops will benefit from protection with cloches or frames and in this case blanching can be effected by covering the frame or cloche with black poly-thene for the last few weeks before harvesting.

Harvesting

Lift and eat the plants as soon as they are sufficiently blanched.

Pests and diseases

Other than a touch of greenfly few problems will be encountered.

Kale (Borecole)

Sow: April to May

Plant: July, August

Harvest: November to May

Kale is a useful crop which can be harvested over a long period and is capable of withstanding the most severe weather. The curly-leaved type (right) is especially popular

A very hardy crop which withstands cold weather well and is a highly nutritious winter vegetable into the bargain.

Selected varieties. Pentland Brigg is an excellent variety which yields a good crop of shoots similar in flavour to the sprouting broccoli. Thousand-headed is another shoot-producing kind, while those grown for their curly leaves include Tall Scotch Curled, Frosty and Hungry Gap.

Soil preparation

Kale is another of the brassica crops and ideally needs a well-firmed, rich soil. However, it is on the whole the easiest of this group of vegetables to grow and will succeed on a poorer soil. A dressing of lime will be needed if the soil is acid and this should be applied in the winter.

Seed sowing

Most of the kales are sown in a separate seedbed in drills 1 cm ($\frac{1}{2}$ in) deep and 23 cm (9 in) apart.

Hungry Gap, however, is sown in its cropping position in early July for cutting in April or May. Sow in rows 45 cm (18 in) apart and thin the young plants to a similar distance.

Planting

The young plants are moved from the seedbed in July and early August and planted 60 cm (2 ft) apart in both directions. Water the seedbed before lifting and plant firmly into moist soil.

Cultivation

As with all vegetables I like to keep the hoe going between the rows throughout the growing season.

Harvesting

There are two sorts, those grown for their leaves and those grown for the young shoots. Both are harvested on a cut-and-come-again basis, the shoots or outer leaves being cut off as required.

Pests and diseases

Kale is subject to the same range of diseases as the other brassicas, see under cabbage.

The young leaves or shoots of Hungry Gap kale are ready for harvesting in spring

Kohl-rabi

Sow: April to August

Harvest: July to November

An unusual vegetable which is becoming increasingly popular in Britain. The swollen stems are the edible portion and I can best describe the rather delicate flavour as being a cross between cabbage and turnip.

Selected varieties. Primavera White, Purple Vienna and White Vienna.

It is important to pull the roots of kohl-rabi before they get too large. This variety is Purple Vienna

Soil preparation

Kohl-rabi should be grown on a soil which has been manured for a previous crop. Dress with general fertilizer at 55 g per square metre (2 oz per square yard) before planting.

Seed sowing

Sow thinly in drills 1 cm ($\frac{1}{2}$ in) deep and 38 cm (15 in) apart and thin the seedlings to 23 cm (9 in). I find that it is important to make sowings at regular intervals to even out the supply as this crop does not stand well.

Cultivation

Water freely in dry weather and hoe regularly to keep down weeds. If necessary feed with a general fertilizer to keep the plants growing.

Harvesting

Pull the roots when they are about the size of tennis balls, if left to grow too large they become tough and stringy.

Storing. Kohl-rabi are best left in the ground and lifted as needed but before they get too large, and this is why it is important to make small successional sowings. They can be lifted and stored in sand or peat in a cool shed but they will not keep very long – a week is about the maximum time I would allow.

Pests and diseases

Although kohl-rabi is one of the brassica crops, few of the usual pests or diseases are encountered, but keep a look out for aphids and club root. See pages 70 to 73.

42

Leeks

Sow: January and February under glass
March out of doors

Plant: May — for plants raised under glass
June — for plants raised out of doors

Harvest: September to May

Leeks, with their mild onion taste, make a pleasant change either served as an individual vegetable or as an ingredient of soups and stews.

Selected varieties. The well-tried favourite Musselburgh is a good reliable variety and Prizetaker is particularly suitable for early sowings made under glass.

Soil preparation

Leeks are a demanding crop as far as the soil is concerned. Well-cultivated ground rich in nutrients and organic matter is much to their liking, and the extra boost given by a dressing of a general fertilizer

Watering newly planted leeks. There is no need to firm them in

Musselburgh is one of the best and most well-known varieties of leek

at the rate of 55 g per square metre (2 oz per square yard) just before sowing or planting out will get them off to a good start.

Seed sowing

To raise an early crop or to grow plants for exhibition, the seeds should be sown in a warm greenhouse in January or February in boxes of John Innes seed compost. Prick out the seedlings when they are large enough to handle into boxes of John Innes potting compost No. 1 or, if they are being grown for exhibition, into 8-cm (3-in) pots. Gradually harden the plants off until May when they can be planted out.

Sow the outdoor crop in March in drills 1 cm ($\frac{1}{2}$ in) deep and 30 cm (12 in) apart.

Planting

Transplant the outdoor-sown plants in June when they are about 15 cm (6 in) high, spacing them 20 to 23 cm (8 to 9 in) apart in rows 30 cm (12 in) apart. The greenhouse-grown seedlings are treated in the same way one month earlier.

To plant the seedlings, make the holes 15 to 20 cm (6 to 8 in) deep with a dibber and drop one plant in each hole. Do not return any soil to the hole, simply water the plants in well.

To raise leeks for exhibition, the seedlings are planted out normally at the same spacing as the other leeks, except that the distance allowed between each row is 45 cm (18 in). The growing programme is slightly different for these, see below.

Cultivation

Hoe well between the rows and water the plants in dry weather.

For exhibition leeks apply a liquid feed every 10 days to ensure maximum development and healthy growth.

Harvesting

Lift the leeks as soon as they are large enough to use, any time from September onwards. They are quite hardy and can be left in the soil right through the winter being lifted as they are required. If the ground they occupy is needed for another crop then lift them and heel them in in another part of the garden.

Pests and diseases

The same range of pests and diseases which attacks the onion can be found on leeks, but generally they are less prone to these troubles.

Lettuce

Sow: January to October

Harvest: All the year round

Lettuces come in many shapes and forms, the two principal kinds being the cabbage and the cos. There are also variations in the leaf texture, some being particularly crisp and brittle.

Selected varieties. A list of these is shown in the suggested cropping plan. My own favourite is the cos Little Gem, which stands well and has a good flavour. Other popular varieties are Continuity and Webb's Wonderful, and for a change the loose-leaved type Salad Bowl which is cropped like spinach.

Soil preparation

This is a crop for which quick growth is essential, so a good but not freshly manured soil is required. Apply a dressing of general fertilizer at 85 g per square metre (3 oz per square yard) before sowing.

Seed sowing

With this crop I would like to stress the importance of sowing a little and often to forestall an unusable surplus of bolting lettuces.

I make the first sowing in late February in pots or boxes under glass. The seedlings are pricked out into peat pots and hardened off for planting out under cloches in late March or early April. When doing this make sure that the rim of the soil ball is covered with garden soil.

For the maincrop sow out of doors at 14-day intervals from March to mid-August, making use of cloches for the earliest of these. The drills need to be 1 cm ($\frac{1}{2}$ in) deep and 30 cm (12 in) apart. Thin the larger varieties to 30 cm (12 in), and the smaller ones, such as Tom Thumb, to 23 cm (9 in).

I find that a good way of getting a succession of plants is to sow half a row and to transplant the thinnings from this to the other

Quick tip

Lamb's lettuce, or corn salad, makes a useful addition to the salad bowl, particularly during the winter. Seeds should be sown in drills 23 cm (9 in) apart and thinned to 10 to 15 cm (4 to 6 in). Choose an area of well-prepared soil and sow in spring for use in the summer and autumn, and again in August or September for use in winter and spring. Harvest the lettuce-like leaves on a cut-and-come-again basis.

Sow	Harvest	Varieties
Late January to February under glass	May to June	Fortune, Unrivalled
March to August	June to October	Continuity, Tom Thumb, All The Year Round, Minetto, Webb's Wonderful, Windermere, Little Gem
Late August in a cold greenhouse	November to December	Kwiek
Mid-October in a cold greenhouse	February to March	Kloek
October in frames	May	Winter Density, Windermere
October to March in frames	March to June	May Queen
September to October out of doors	April to May	Valdor, Arctic King, Imperial Winter

Above An all-the-year-round cropping plan for lettuce

It is important to sow lettuce seed thinly and a little at a time

Thin the seedlings and transplant the thinnings to give a later crop

Cloches can be used to produce lettuces out of the normal season

44

half of the row. The transplanted seedlings will come to maturity some two weeks later than the others.

Some varieties can be sown from late August to mid-October for harvesting in winter and spring. These sowings can take place in a cold greenhouse, garden frame, or out of doors depending on which variety is used.

Cultivation

Lettuces must be grown without a check, so be generous with the water. Nothing causes lettuces to

Lettuce is a vegetable which comes in a variety of forms and textures and the main ones are shown here. **1.** Cos. **2.** Cabbage — probably the most popular kind. **3.** Crisphead, well named for its crisp and brittle leaf texture. **4.** The loose-leaved kind such as Salad Bowl

1

2

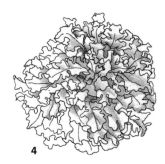

3

Lettuces bolt quickly once they reach maturity; sow only as many as you need

run to seed more quickly than poor soil and dry conditions.

Those which are to be over-wintered without protection must have a warm, sheltered position. I keep the slugs away by putting down slug pellets in late autumn and early spring, and speed up cropping by covering with cloches.

In March, feed winter lettuces with a general fertilizer at 55 g per square metre (2 oz to the square yard); this can be sprinkled along the row and hoed in, but take care to keep it off the leaves.

Lettuces grown under glass should be planted shallowly as damping off may occur if the lowest leaves are not above soil level.

Harvesting

Pull when the heart is firm to the touch.

Putting down slug pellets

Pests and diseases

Mildew and botrytis (grey mould) are the diseases to watch for, and if the conditions are to their liking they will spread quickly.

Pests come in the form of aphids, slugs or cutworms. See pages 70 to 73.

Other troubles. Crops which refuse to heart up indicate that the soil lacks either firmness or organic matter, or both. Bolting — plants running up to seed — happens as soon as the plants reach maturity, so it is important not to sow at any one time more than you can use.

45

Marrow

Sow: April under glass
May out of doors

Harvest: July to September

There are two main kinds of marrow: the bush type which is the most suitable for smaller gardens and includes the popular courgettes, and the trailing kind.

Selected varieties. Tender and True is a favourite bush variety. Others include Green Bush Improved and White Bush, the courgettes Zucchini F₁, and Green Bush, and the attractive Golden Zucchini, the fruits of which can be eaten as courgettes or allowed to grow to full size.

Trailing kinds are Long White Trailing, Long Green Trailing, Table Dainty and Little Gem. The last has small round fruits and will

Green Bush Improved is one of the most popular varieties of bush marrow

climb happily up a tripod or wall and so save valuable space.

There are also some unusual types which are worth a try. These include the custard marrows, bush varieties with round, flattened fruits with scalloped edges, and Vegetable Spaghetti, a trailing kind with oval fruits which are boiled whole and then cut open to reveal the flesh which comes away from the skin like spaghetti.

Soil preparation

A sunny position and good soil containing well-rotted manure or compost are the basic requirements. I find that the best method of preparation is to make a hole 60 cm (2 ft) wide and deep for each plant then to refill this with compost or manure to within 23 cm (9 in) of the top. Cover the manure with soil taken from the hole, building it up to form a mound, and leave a saucer-like depression on the top to make watering easier.

Seed sowing

A temperature of around 18°C (65°F) is required for germination

and I like to sow two seeds in each 9-cm (3½-in) pot and then thin the seedlings to leave the strongest in each pot.

Outdoor sowings must wait until mid-May and the seeds should then be covered with cloches or upturned jam jars until they have germinated. Sow the seeds in twos, 2·5 cm (1 in) deep, and allow 1 m (3 ft) between plants for bush varieties and 1·25 m (4 ft) or more for the trailing kinds. Thin to leave one plant (the strongest) at each position.

Quick tip

Why not utilize the compost heap for a few months to grow marrows? Simply place 15 cm (6 in) of soil over the top of the heap and sow the seeds as already described. Choose a bush variety.

Top Male (left) and female (right) marrow flowers. *Above* Pollinating the female flower

Planting a marrow First make a hole about 60 cm (2 ft) deep and the same measurement across

Next, spread a layer of well-rotted compost or manure in the hole and replace the soil to form a slight mound

The young marrow plant is placed in a saucer-shaped depression on top of the mound of soil

Cultivation

The pot-grown seedlings are ready for planting out in early June at the spacings already given and I think that it is advisable to cover them with cloches for the first week. Trailing varieties need a certain amount of training – the ends of the runners should be pinched out when they have grown to 1 m (3 ft). This encourages the production of side shoots which usually carry the female flowers. These shoots can be reduced in number if necessary. Trailing varieties planted in frames will need pinching out at 45 cm (18 in).

Bush varieties require no such training.

Although insects can usually be expected to carry out pollination I find that it is a good idea to make sure of this with the early varieties by hand pollination. Do this by removing the male flowers (the ones with thin stalks), pulling off the petals and dusting the pollen from the central core into the middle of the female flower. Marrows grown under glass will always need to be hand pollinated.

Marrows must have plenty of water at all times and will need feeding with weak liquid manure when the first fruits start to swell. Hoe regularly.

It is possible to grow the trailing varieties up some form of support or trellis and in this way they will take less room. However, this is really only practicable with the small-fruited sorts and I suggest a variety such as Little Gem for this sort of treatment.

Harvesting

Cut the marrows when they are small and before the skins become tough. Courgettes should be about 10 to 15 cm (4 to 6 in) long.

Storing. If marrows are allowed to reach full size and become fully ripe before cutting, they can be stored in net or string bags in a frostproof place.

Pests and diseases

Watch out for aphid and slug attack. The main diseases are grey mould (particularly in a wet season), mildew and mosaic. See pages 70 to 73.

Mosaic is a virus disease which causes yellow blotches or mottling on the leaves, and fruits will fail to grow properly. There is no cure and the best course of action is to destroy affected plants.

Courgettes, both green and yellow kinds, are a type of bush marrow

Mustard and Cress

Sow: April to August out of doors
All the year round under glass

Harvest: All the year round

Easily and rapidly grown, the mixture of mustard and cress is popular both as a salad vegetable and as a garnish.

Selected varieties. The seed of these two plants is bought separately, and that is how I like to grow them; mixing the seedlings when they are cut rather than sowing them both in the same container. White Mustard and Curled Cress are the most popular varieties but I suggest you give Super Salad cress a try – it will remain in a fresh condition for several days when it is ready for cutting whereas the curled types will go over quite quickly.

Soil preparation

The seed can be sown in the open ground, in which case it is very lightly covered, or indoors on a window ledge, or in a greenhouse. Indoors the seed is sown on moist peat, flannel or blotting paper and no covering is necessary except a sheet of glass and brown paper. The nutritional value of the soil is unimportant as the young plants are harvested so rapidly.

Seed sowing

Sow the seed broadcast, whether indoors or out, on the moist seed-bed – water is the only requirement of the plants up until the time they are cut. Indoor crops should be sown on the medium chosen in shallow trays or boxes and the glass and brown paper should be removed as soon as the seeds germinate. Cress is slower growing than mustard and for this reason is always sown three days earlier so that the two plants are ready for cutting at the same time. A germination temperature of 13°C (55°F) is desirable for both crops.

Cultivation

Water the seedlings regularly throughout their short growing period.

Harvesting

The mustard and cress can be cut and mixed as soon as the seedlings are 5 to 8 cm (2 to 3 in) high. As this is a crop which does not stand well small amounts of seed should be sown at regular intervals.

Pests and diseases

The crop is harvested at such an early age that the only problem is likely to be damping off. See page 72.

Mustard (right) and cress (left) are easily grown. Remember to sow the cress three days earlier than the mustard

Onions

Sow: December and January under glass
March, August and September out of doors

Plant: March or April

Harvest: June onwards

The onion, in its various forms, is one of the most valuable crops grown in the garden. One of its most useful characteristics is that it is always in season.

Selected varieties. The range of onions available is nothing short of bewildering, but if you stick to the following varieties you will not go far wrong. For the earliest sowings under glass Ailsa Craig is my personal favourite, while for spring sowing Bedfordshire Champion and Primodoro will give good-sized bulbs. For autumn sowings Solidity and Autumn Queen are reliable, but the Japanese varieties such as Express Yellow and Senshyu are especially recommended.

Soil preparation

Onions must have a sunny site if they are to ripen properly so give them an open situation. The fattest and tastiest crops are grown on well-cultivated land which has been well manured the previous autumn or winter. Dig in whatever is available in the way of organic matter, whether it is well-rotted stable or farmyard manure or just good garden compost. I find that ash from the bonfire forked into the top few inches of soil together with a light dressing of bonemeal – between 55 and 110 g per square metre (2 to 4 oz per square yard) – gives them a good start.

Seed sowing

The earliest sowings are carried out under glass in a temperature of 13 to 16°C (55 to 60°F). Sow the seeds thinly in boxes of seed compost.

When the seedlings are 5 to 8 cm (2 to 3 in) tall, they should be potted up into 9-cm (3½-in) pots and gradually hardened off for planting out in mid-April. This method of raising is usually adopted if the onions are being grown for exhibition as they mature that much faster.

The maincrop onions are sown outdoors in March in drills 1 cm (½ in) deep and 30 cm (12 in) apart. The soil should be raked down to a fine tilth and firmed well before sowing.

Autumn sowings, to provide a summer crop, are made in sheltered seedbeds, the seedlings being transplanted the following March.

For all these crops the seedlings are planted or thinned to give a spacing of 15 cm (6 in) between the plants. For exhibition onions 23 cm (9 in) will allow more room for the bulbs to develop.

Planting

Perhaps the easiest way of growing onions is to raise them from small bulbs or sets. These are planted in March or April 15 cm (6 in) apart in rows 30 cm (12 in) apart. Plant the bulbs just underneath the surface of the soil – they will push themselves up as the roots begin to form.

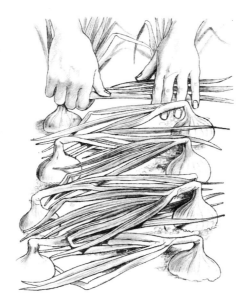

When onions are ready for harvesting growth slows down and the foliage withers; the tops should be bent over if this does not happen naturally

Lifting the onions and turn them upside down to allow the underneaths to dry out

Cultivation

Regular hoeing is necessary to keep down weed growth and the plants should be watered well when the soil shows signs of drying out. Should the ground become too dry then the onions will stop growing and start to ripen. Remove any flower heads as they form and apply a liquid fertilizer every ten days throughout the growing season. When growth slows down and the onions are of a good size, bend over the tops, if this does not happen naturally, to allow the sun to ripen the bulbs.

Harvesting

Lift the bulbs with a fork as soon as they are fully developed, turn them upside down and allow them to dry out on the surface of the soil for a few days. If the weather is particularly wet, lay them out in an airy shed, a cold frame or on the greenhouse staging.

Storing. As soon as they are ripe and dry (usually two to three weeks after lifting) the onions can either be plaited into strings or tied in bundles and stored in an airy, frostproof place. Only sound, undamaged onions should be stored; any which are bruised, cut or diseased will quickly rot.

Pests and diseases

Eelworm and onion fly are the two pests most likely to cause trouble. Of the diseases, mildew, white rot and neck rot are the most common. See pages 70 to 73.

Other troubles. The plants may bolt if seed is sown too early when the weather is excessively cold.

Spring onions

A variety such as White Lisbon sown thinly in drills in August will give you a crop of salad onions for harvesting in spring. There is no need to thin – just pull the onions at intervals along the row as you need them. Sowings made from March onwards will extend their season of use to the summer and autumn months.

Some fine examples of Ailsa Craig

Welsh onions

This onion differs from the rest in that it is perennial and forms swollen stem bases rather than bulbs. Sown from February to May it will give summer onions which can be used in the same way as spring onions. Each plant will produce a clump of these fat stems and for this reason should be divided every three years and the offsets replanted individually.

Shallots

Planted like onion sets, but earlier in the season – from February to March – shallots will grow like the Welsh onion in clusters. Harvest them from July onwards in the

same way as you would ordinary onions and rub off the loose outer skins before storing. Keep some firm, healthy bulbs aside for replanting the following spring. Longkeeping Yellow and Giant Yellow are well-tried varieties which can be used for cooking or pickling.

Pickling onions

These are smaller varieties of the ordinary onion which lend themselves, by virtue of their size and flavour, to being pickled. The Queen, Paris Silver-skin and Cocktail are all worth growing, and the last two are very quick to mature.

50

Parsnips

Sow: Early March to May

Harvest: September onwards

Though they are not to everybody's taste as an individual vegetable, parsnips are very useful as an addition to stews and casseroles.

Selected varieties. My favourite varieties are Tender and True and Hollow Crown.

Soil preparation

Like all root vegetables, parsnips require a well-cultivated soil but not one which has been freshly manured. I find that a general fertilizer applied at the rate of 55 g per square metre (2 oz per square yard) is sufficient for their requirements.

Seed sowing

Sow the seeds in groups of two or three 23 cm (9 in) apart in drills 2·5 cm (1 in) deep and 45 cm (18 in) apart. Germination can be rather slow.

Remove all but one seedling from each group as soon as they are large enough to handle.

When harvesting parsnips use a fork to loosen the soil before pulling the roots

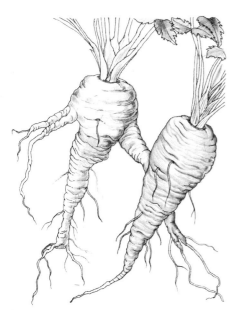

Manured or stony soil gives rise to branched roots, as shown on the left

Cultivation

Hoe between the rows regularly and weed between the individual plants.

Harvesting

Lift the roots from September onwards as they are required.

Storing. I recommend that you lift a fair proportion of the crop in November and store the roots in boxes of sand or peat in a sheltered place out of doors or in a cool shed or garage. The remainder of the crop may be left in the ground until as late as February – frost will greatly improve their flavour – but the batch you lifted will save you trying to dig up roots from hard frozen soil until it is absolutely necessary.

Pests and diseases

The main problem with parsnips is a disease called canker which causes the roots to crack and rot. Carrot fly attack may leave the roots open to infection by this disease and due care should be taken to control this pest. Cracking of the roots after heavy rain, or a surplus of nitrogen in the soil, can also weaken them and leave them open to attack. Some varieties show a marked resistance to the disease. See pages 70 to 73.

Other troubles. Forking of the roots may occur in heavily manured soils.

Quick tip

On very heavy or stony ground make 45- to 60-cm (18- to 24-in) deep holes with a crowbar, fill them with a mixture of soil, peat and a little bonemeal and sow the seeds on top. The parsnips which result will be long and tender.

Peas

Sow: January to February under glass
March to late June and in October out of doors

Harvest: June to October

The large number of pea varieties may make the decision of which to grow somewhat difficult. It is important to maintain a succession of cropping.

Selected varieties. I start with Feltham First, then Little Marvel, Kelvedon Wonder and Early Onward. Onward and Dwarf Defiance are good maincrop choices and Kelvedon Wonder sows well in succession throughout the summer.

Soil preparation

Peas need a deeply dug soil which has been well manured in the autumn or winter. Rake in a dressing of general fertilizer before sowing and add lime if the soil is acid.

Onward is one of the most useful of maincrop pea varieties

Seed sowing

The first sowing under glass can be made in late January and for this I use the variety Feltham First, placing three or four seeds in each 9-cm (3½-in) pot. The young plants are hardened off for planting outside in late March or early April depending on weather conditions – cloche protection may be required.

Sowing peas in a trench

Out of doors the first sowings are made in March, or late February under cloches. Further sowings can then follow at fortnightly intervals.

It is possible to sow a variety such as Meteor at the end of October to give an early crop the following spring, but cloche protection may be required.

All outdoor sowings are made in a flat-bottomed trench 5 cm (2 in) deep and 20 cm (8 in) wide, the seeds being placed 8 cm (3 in)

Quick tip

For something different, why not try the sugar pea variety Carouby de Maussane. Sown in succession from March to June the flat pods are picked and cooked whole.

apart. The distance between successive rows should be equivalent to the eventual height of the variety grown.

Cultivation

Hoe regularly and water well in dry weather. Provide some form of support (pea sticks, netting, etc.) as soon as the tendrils form.

This is another crop where moisture is all important for good results and I find that a mulch of peat or similar organic matter is helpful in maintaining the moisture content of the soil.

Harvesting

Pick regularly as soon as the pods are well filled.

Pests and diseases

Mice, pigeons and slugs are all attracted by the seeds while pea moth, pea weevil, aphids and thrips will attack the plants and developing pods.

Mildew, a fungus disease, is likely to be a problem in a dry season and on the later sowings.

See pages 70 to 73.

Other troubles. Failure of the pods to fill may be caused by either cool showery weather or hot, dry conditions at flowering time which lead to incomplete pollination. Another reason may be too much nitrogen in the soil causing the production of leaves at the expense of the pods.

Peppers

Sow: March under glass

Plant: Early June

Harvest: August onwards

Both the sweet pepper or capsicum, a valuable addition to salads and casseroles, and the chilli or hot pepper, used in pickles and sauces, are grown in exactly the same way.

Selected varieties. New Ace, Worldbeater and Canapé are good varieties of sweet pepper; chillies are generally sold as 'mixed'.

Soil preparation

Although I feel that it is more satisfactory to grow peppers under glass, they can be grown out of doors through the summer where a greenhouse is not available. In such circumstances a sheltered spot in full sun should be found for them where the soil is light and not too rich in organic matter. In very rich soils peppers will produce more foliage than fruits.

Seed sowing

Sow the seeds in a warm greenhouse and, as soon as the seedlings are large enough to handle, pot them up into 8-cm (3-in) pots. If the plants are to be grown out of doors they should be gradually hardened off until the end of May.

Quick tip

This is another crop which does well in peat bags, and this is an easy way of growing them on the patio or even in the conservatory. Allow three plants to each bag.

New Ace, a variety of the sweet pepper or capsicum

Plants which are to be grown in the greenhouse should be potted on into 15-cm (6-in) pots of John Innes potting compost No. 3 as soon as they have outgrown the smaller pots.

Planting

The outdoor crop should be planted 45 cm (18 in) apart in both directions and each plant should be given a stout cane. The indoor crop will also need staking.

Cultivation

Pinch out the tip of each plant when it is 15 cm (6 in) high and give regular liquid feeds – once a fortnight is sufficient – as soon as

the fruit starts to set. Hoe between the outdoor plants and ensure that they have a plentiful supply of water.

Harvesting

As the peppers ripen they change colour to yellow and red but the immature green ones can also be used, in fact they are usually marketed at this stage. Do pick regularly as this will encourage the production of more fruits.

Pests and diseases

Red spider mite may be a problem with greenhouse-grown peppers and greenfly will attack both indoor and outdoor crops. See page 70.

Potatoes

Plant: March (early)
April (mid-season and late)

Harvest: June to July (early)
August onwards (mid-season and late)

The space and trouble taken in growing potatoes is, I feel, always amply repaid by the delicious flavour of the first early crop brought to the table.

Selected varieties. Of the earlies, Arran Pilot, Home Guard, and Epicure are good, though personally I find Sharpe's Express more tasty. For maincrop growing the mainstay must surely be Majestic which will give a good crop on most soils. Pentland Crown, Pentland Dell and King Edward VII are also worth growing.

Soil preparation

For potatoes to grow well and produce tubers of a reasonable size, a rich, well-worked soil which has the ability to retain moisture is needed.

Preparation of the ground should start in the autumn before planting. Dig the land to at least one spade's depth and incorporate well-rotted farmyard or stable manure or good garden compost. Sandy soils in particular should be given plenty of organic matter to help the retention of water, without which the tubers will be underdeveloped and few in number. The following spring, immediately before planting, give the soil a good dressing of a general fertilizer – 55 g per square metre (2 oz per square yard) will be sufficient – and work this into the top few inches with a fork.

Potatoes have a well-deserved reputation for breaking down heavy clay soils by the action of their roots; nevertheless, they should be given every assistance by adequate cultivation and application of organic matter.

Preparation of the tubers

Potato crops are grown from potato tubers which are sold as 'seed' potatoes. The important thing about seed potatoes is that they are certified free from virus diseases which, if present, would seriously reduce the subsequent yield. It is possible to save and replant tubers from your own crops, but I do not recommend this practice as it is all too easy to get a major outbreak of disease if the tubers are infected. It is far better to buy fresh certified seed each year.

To prepare them for planting the seed potatoes are best if sprouted or 'chitted'. This involves placing them eye end uppermost in seedboxes and keeping them in a light, frostproof place until each eye produces a shoot. When these shoots are about 4 cm (1½ in) long the tubers are ready for planting, and I like to rub off all but the three strongest shoots from each tuber before doing this.

Planting

For the earliest crops the tubers can be planted in late February or early March but be sure to choose a sheltered position. In more open situations, plant at the end of March when there is less risk of the crop being damaged by extreme weather conditions.

Plant the tubers 30 cm (12 in) apart in 'V'-shaped trenches 13 cm (5 in) deep; this makes earthing up easier and more effective. Be sure to leave at least 60 cm (2 ft) between the rows to allow the plants to develop fully.

Maincrop varieties will make larger plants and for this reason they will need more room. I find that 38 to 45 cm (15 to 18 in) between tubers and 75 cm (2½ ft) between rows is a suitable spacing.

Cultivation

As soon as the sprouts appear, draw some soil over them to give protection against frost. Earthing up should continue regularly now –

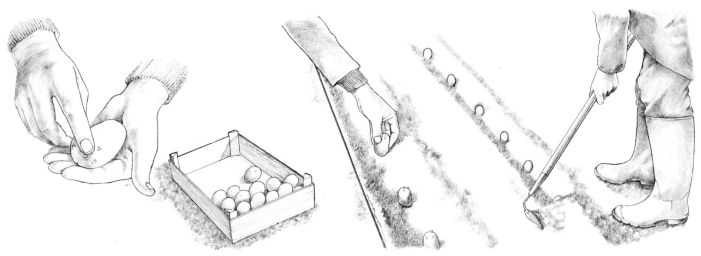

Seed potatoes should be chitted by putting them eye end uppermost in seedboxes and keeping them in a light place

Take out a V-shaped trench and plant the chitted potatoes at the spacings given in the text

Cover with soil. As soon as the sprouts appear earth them up by drawing some more soil over them

Choose a dry day for harvesting potatoes. If they are to be stored then leave the tubers on the surface of the soil for a few hours to dry

hessian sacks and store them in a cool dark place which is frostproof.

Pests and diseases

Slugs, wireworms and eelworms are the pests most likely to be encountered. Of the diseases, virus infections, potato blight, wart disease and scab are the most serious. See pages 70 to 73.

Other troubles. If potatoes are grown on excessively chalky soils, the tubers may be waxy in texture and of a very poor flavour. If your soil is rather alkaline try growing Home Guard as an early crop and Majestic for maincrop supplies – these two varieties are more amenable to growing on chalk than many others.

soil being drawn up around the stems as they emerge – allowing only the top few inches of the shoots to remain visible. As well as blanching the tubers, regular earthing up will also keep down weeds.

In early July the foliage of potatoes should be sprayed as a preventive against blight. Use either Bordeaux mixture or another copper fungicide and spray thoroughly.

Forcing. If, like me, you like eating home-grown potatoes at the earliest possible opportunity, you may like to try forcing some in January in pots in a warm greenhouse. Use large pots for this – five sprouted potatoes will fit in a 23- or 25-cm (9- or 10-in) pot and three in a 18- or 20-cm (7- or 8-in) pot. I find that a little peat mixed with John Innes potting compost No. 3 gives the tubers just what they want in the way of nutrition and moisture. Fill the pot halfway and plant the tubers 5 cm (2 in) deep. As the sprouts grow, topdress gradually with the same compost mixture until the soil level is about 2·5 cm (1 in) below the rim of the

pot. With good light and adequate watering the tubers will be ready for eating in mid-April, and, believe me, they will taste delicious.

Harvesting

The early potatoes grown in the open will be ready for lifting in June or July – a time which generally coincides with flowering. If you are not sure that they are ready, lift one plant as an experiment; you can always eat the tubers even if they are small and you will then know the state of the rest.

Lift the tubers of the earlies as you want to use them. The maincrop varieties should be lifted from August onwards. In October, choose a fine day and lift any remaining tubers, leaving them on the surface of the soil for a few hours to dry.

Storing. Store only those tubers which are sound and undamaged. Should a damaged or decaying potato be included the rot may spread to other tubers. Place the tubers carefully into paper or

Quick tip

For potatoes with a difference plant the salad potato Pink Fir Apple in mid-April. Cultivation is the same as other potatoes and the result will be a supply of long, knobbly pink tubers – superb in winter salads.

Pumpkins

Sow: April under glass
Late May out of doors

Harvest: September

Pumpkins need a lot of space and are not the ideal crop for small gardens although you may consider that the fun of growing them tends to outweigh this disadvantage.
Selected varieties. Hubbard Squash Golden, Hundredweight (the largest variety).

Soil preparation

Pumpkins are heavy feeders and it will be necessary to supply well-rotted compost or manure in quantity – a barrowload to each plant if possible. Although the pumpkin does require plenty of room it will grow in a partially shaded position and this may make it easier to find a suitable site.

For each plant dig a hole about 45 cm (1½ ft) deep. Fill this to within 15 cm (6 in) of the top with compost or manure and finish off with 15 cm (6 in) of soil.

Seed sowing

Sow the seeds in pots or boxes under glass and harden off for planting out in late May. They will need to be set out 2 m (6 ft) apart.

Alternatively, sow the seed out of doors, placing two in each cropping position and thinning to leave the sturdiest one on each site.

Cultivation

The care of plants is similar to that required for the marrow, copious watering and regular feeding being especially important.

I find that four fruits are sufficient for each plant to ripen but if you are aiming at the giant size for Harvest Festivals then you should allow only one or two to develop. As soon as the fruits reach their maximum size cut down the watering and stop feeding. This will encourage the fruit to ripen.

Harvesting and storing

Cut in September and allow the fruits to dry off. Store in a dry frost-proof place.

Pests and diseases

Keep a look out for slugs, snails and mice, all of which have a liking for the developing fruits. See page 70.

Quick tip

It is a good idea to turn the fruits fairly frequently; this will help to keep them a good shape and encourage them to colour evenly.

Pumpkins make a large amount of growth and are only suitable for larger gardens

Radish

Sow: February – under frames or cloches
March to mid-August – out of doors

Harvest: April to September
Autumn and winter (winter radish)

The crisp, hot-tasting radish will liven up any salad and is a favourite of the impatient gardener – the summer-sown crops giving edible roots in less than a month.

Selected varieties. For early crops under frames or cloches I suggest Red Forcing or French Breakfast Forcing, while for main-crop sowings why not try Cherry Belle, French Breakfast or Sparkler? I find China Rose and Black Spanish Round to be the best of the winter radish.

Soil preparation

If the radishes are to grow fast and produce crisp roots and not run to seed they must be sown in a rich, moist soil. Apply a dressing of general fertilizer at 55 g per square metre (2 oz per square yard) before sowing to get the crop off to a good start.

Seed sowing

The fact that radish are fast growing makes them a very versatile crop. They can be sown in drills between other slower maturing crops such as lettuce, onions, or – and I prefer to do this – between celery trenches. Sow the seed thinly in drills 1 cm ($\frac{1}{2}$ in) deep and 15 cm (6 in) apart (if you are not inter-cropping) and sow either in short rows or a section of a long row at two-week intervals to give a succession.

The winter radish forms a much larger root and is sliced rather than served whole. Sowings can be made in July, this time leaving 30 cm (12 in) between the rows and thinning the plants to leave one every 20 cm (8 in).

China Rose is one of the larger radish varieties and can be grown for use in the winter

Cultivation

Hoe between the rows regularly and ensure that the crop has an adequate supply of water to speed up the fattening of the roots.

Quick tip

Try mixing the seed with an equal amount of lettuce seed and sowing in a drill 1 cm ($\frac{1}{2}$ in) deep. The radishes will be ready well before the lettuce and when they are pulled the lettuce crop is automatically thinned.

Harvesting

Pull the roots regularly as soon as they are large enough to eat. If left in the ground too long they will become woody and unpalatable.

The winter radish can also be pulled when they are of a good size – much larger than the summer types. A number of roots can be pulled at once and stored in boxes of dry sand, alternatively they can be left in the ground – with the protection of a layer of bracken or straw – and pulled when required.

Pests and diseases

Flea beetle is the most common cause of trouble, see page 70.

Other troubles. If not grown very quickly the radishes will lose their flavour and become very hard.

Rhubarb

Sow: March under glass
April out of doors

Plant: March

Harvest: January to March if forced
April to July in natural season

Rhubarb, with its highly individual flavour, is a welcome ingredient of pies, jams and chutneys. The leaf stalks are the edible part and this is why it is classed as a vegetable and not as a fruit.

Selected varieties. Holstein Bloodred, Champagne and Victoria are all reliable.

Soil preparation

All too often rhubarb is given a home in a dark corner of the garden in a soil which any other vegetable would find unacceptable. And yet rhubarb is more demanding than many of these if it is to do really well. To get the best crops give it a deeply worked soil which has been well manured, and a site which gets plenty of sun.

Seed sowing

It is possible to raise rhubarb from seed if a good strain is selected and the seeds sown either in a frame in March or out of doors in drills 2·5 cm (1 in) deep and 30 cm (12 in) apart in April. Thin the seedlings to leave a strong young plant every 15 cm (6 in). The plants are removed to their cropping position the following autumn.

Planting

Planting of young crowns, available from most nurserymen, is carried out in March. Insert them 5 cm (2 in) below the surface of the soil and at a spacing of 1 m (3 ft) to give each of them room to develop. In a small garden there may only be room for one clump.

Cultivation

Do not pull any sticks during the first year – this gives the plant time to establish itself and produce a good root system and a larger crown. Remove flowers whenever they form. Topdress in February each year using manure or garden compost.

Forcing. Rhubarb can be forced either in situ or in boxes brought into sheds or greenhouses. To force out of doors simply cover the crowns in January with boxes or barrels, insulating these with piles of leaves or manure. The sticks can be pulled as soon as they are of a reasonable size – they will be ready about a month earlier than usual.

To crop plants in January and February they must be forced in boxes under protection. Lift several strong roots in November, expose them to the frost for a few days and then plant them close together in boxes of light soil. The soil should be moist and the boxes kept in a warm place and covered with sacks to keep out the light. If a temperature of 13 to 24°C (55 to 75°F) is maintained the sticks will be ready for picking in five to seven weeks. The crowns which have been used for forcing indoors should be discarded afterwards.

Harvesting

The sticks of the natural season rhubarb can be pulled until July; the plants should then be given a chance to build up reserves for the following year. I like to give an application of general fertilizer at 55 g per square metre (2 oz per square yard) when picking is finished.

Lift and divide the crowns every four years.

Pests and diseases

Crown rot is the only problem likely to be encountered. See page 72.

This rhubarb has been blanched under a specially made pot; however, boxes, tubs, or old buckets can equally well be used for this purpose

Salsify and Scorzonera

Sow: Salsify — April and May
Scorzonera — May

Harvest: Salsify — October
Scorzonera — September onwards

Salsify and scorzonera, with their distinctive flavour of oysters, are two root vegetables which deserve to be more widely grown.

Selected varieties. Sutton's Giant and Mammoth Sandwich Island are good varieties of salsify, and Russian Giant of scorzonera.

Soil preparation

The roots are long and slender and for this reason they need a deeply cultivated soil which is relatively free of stones. Land which has been manured for a previous crop is ideal and I give a dusting of general fertilizer at the rate of 55 g per square metre (2 oz per square yard) before sowing.

Salsify is grown mainly for its long oyster-flavoured roots and needs a good, deeply cultivated soil. The leaves can, however, be picked for use in salads

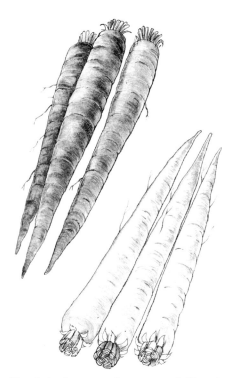

The distinctive roots of scorzonera (left) and salsify (right)

Seed sowing

Sow the seeds in drills 2·5 cm (1 in) deep and 38 cm (15 in) apart. As an alternative, the 'crowbar' method described for parsnips may be used on heavy or stony ground.

Thin the seedlings as soon as they can be handled easily, leaving one every 23 cm (9 in).

Cultivation

An occasional light hoeing between the rows is all that is necessary.

Harvesting

Lift the roots for use from September onwards. On heavy soils the roots may all be lifted in one go for storage.

Storing. The roots can be stored in boxes of dry sand or peat in a cool garage or shed after lifting, great care being taken not to break or in any way damage them. On light soils some roots may be left in the ground until they are needed.

Pests and diseases

These vegetables are not particularly badly affected by pests and diseases.

Other troubles. Heavily manured or stony ground will cause the roots to fork. Seeds of scorzonera sown before May have a tendency to bolt.

Quick tip

To prevent wastage, sow the seeds in clumps of 3 or 4 at intervals of 23 cm (9 in) and thin to leave the strongest seedling in each group.

Seakale

Plant: March to April

Harvest: December to March

Cuttings can be made from the side roots of the seakale crowns

When potting up the crowns allow the tops to show above the surface

This very delicious vegetable is not widely grown but it is not difficult and is well worth a try. The young blanched shoots are the edible part.

Soil preparation

A well-dug and very well-manured soil is required; if it is acid then apply a light dressing of hydrated lime before planting.

Cultivation

In March or April plant the root cuttings (also known as thongs) so that their tops are 1 cm ($\frac{1}{2}$ in) below the soil surface. The method

The blanched shoots of seakale which have been forced under pots out of doors

of preparing the cuttings is described below.

Hoe regularly. Water when dry, and feed occasionally. When the young shoots appear remove the smallest and weakest to leave one on each root.

By November the roots will have formed strong crowns and will be ready for lifting. Trim the side roots close to the main root and prepare these as root cuttings; they should be 10 to 13 cm (4 to 5 in) long with the upper ends cut straight across and the lower ends slanting. This will help you to recognize which end is which when

planting time comes round. Tie the root cuttings in bundles and store them in a sheltered place for planting the following spring.

The crowns, from which the cuttings have been taken, are put in a sheltered position out of doors and covered with sand. They can then be forced, a few at a time, at regular intervals. To do this pot them up in boxes or 20-cm (8-in) pots allowing about 10 cm (4 in) between the crowns, which should just show above the surface of the compost. Bring the pots into a warm greenhouse, temperature 10 to 13°C (50 to 55°F), and make sure that they are kept completely dark by covering them with black polythene or a box. The shoots are ready for cutting when they are 15 to 23 cm (6 to 9 in) long and this takes some 4 to 5 weeks to achieve.

In January any crowns still remaining out of doors can be forced in situ by putting boxes or pots over them.

Seakale can also be raised from seed sown in April in drills 2·5 cm (1 in) deep and 30 cm (12 in) apart. Thin the seedlings to 15 cm (6 in) and plant out in their permanent site the following February or March. It takes two years before plants raised from seed are strong enough to force.

Harvesting

Cut each shoot with a small piece of the crown and take the outer ones first.

Pests and diseases

Seakale is fairly free from pest and disease problems.

Spinach

Sow: Summer kind Mid-March to mid-July
Winter kind August to September

Harvest: Summer kind May to October
Winter kind October to April

It is possible to obtain a year-round supply of spinach by growing both the winter and summer kinds. This is a crop which does not like hot, dry conditions and needs to be grown quickly.

Selected varieties. Long-standing Round is a summer-cropping variety, Long-standing Prickly and Broad-leaved Prickly winter cropping. Such varieties as Greenmarket and Sigmaleaf are suitable for both spring and early autumn sowing.

Soil preparation

A sunny or partially shaded position which is sheltered in the winter is the best, and the soil should be well worked, manured and dressed with lime if it is acid. Topdress with a general fertilizer before sowing.

Seed sowing

Sow thinly in drills 2·5 cm (1 in) deep and 30 cm (12 in) apart. Thin

Gather spinach a few leaves at a time

Long-standing Round is one of the best varieties for spring and summer sowing

to 23 cm (9 in) for the summer kind and 10 cm (4 in) for the winter. It is particularly important to sow the summer spinach in small quantities as it will not stand long after reaching its peak.

Cultivation

Water well in dry weather. In cooler areas protect winter spinach with cloches or straw in cold weather.

Harvesting

Gather a few leaves from each plant as soon as they are a usable size, and continue to pick in this way, always taking the outside leaves.

Pests and diseases

Birds and slugs seem to be the main problem, see page 70.

Other troubles. The tendency of the crop to bolt in hot weather can be reduced by good soil preparation, plenty of water and frequent hoeing to keep down competition from weeds.

Quick tip

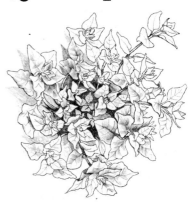

For a change why not try New Zealand spinach? This rather succulent plant with a trailing habit and fleshy leaves is not a true spinach and is particularly useful in hot, dry conditions as it stands lack of water well.

Sow under glass in mid-April, outside in May. Harvest by picking the tips of the shoots and the leaves.

61

Swede

Sow: May or June

Harvest: October onwards

The swede is a valuable winter root crop but its strong, distinctive flavour is an acquired taste.

Selected varieties. Purple Top and Bronze Top are good, well-tried varieties, and the new Chignecto has the advantage of showing a marked resistance to club root.

Soil preparation

A well-cultivated soil manured for a previous crop is best for growing swedes, and an application of a general fertilizer at the rate of 55 g per square metre (2 oz per square yard) will get them off to a good start if applied just before sowing.

Seed sowing

Sow the seeds in 1-cm ($\frac{1}{2}$-in) deep drills, leaving 38 cm (15 in) between the rows. Thin the seedlings when they are 5 cm (2 in) high leaving one plant every 23 cm (9 in).

Quick tip

Swedes make a useful catch crop to follow early potatoes, peas or broad beans. Apply a dressing of general fertilizer and sow thinly in June or July.

Cultivation

Keep down weeds by hoeing between the rows and in dry weather make sure that water is freely available – swedes are a thirsty crop.

Harvesting

Lift the roots as they are needed from October onwards and in December, in all but the very mildest areas, all the remaining roots should be lifted for storing. In mild climates the roots can be left in the ground and pulled as required.

Storing. Remove the leaves as close to the crown as possible without actually cutting into the root, and remove also the thin tail end of the root. Swedes, like carrots, can be stored in boxes of dry sand in a frostproof place.

Pests and diseases

Swedes are attacked by almost the same pests and diseases as turnips, but one disease – brown heart – is more prevalent in swedes.

Swedes are a valuable winter root crop and Purple Top, which is shown here, is a good variety

Sweet Corn

Sow: April under glass
May out of doors

Plant: Late May for plants raised under glass

Harvest: Early August to late October

By growing a few plants of sweet corn you can bring something a little exotic to the garden; the sight and taste of hot cobs running with butter will make the effort of growing them well worthwhile.

Selected varieties. For early-maturing sweet corn try First of All and Earliking, and for the rest of the season Kelvedon Glory, John Innes Hybrid and Golden Bantam will give a good crop. If you live in a cooler part of the country North Star is a variety which might be more suited to your conditions.

Soil preparation

A sunny site is essential if the cobs of sweet corn are to ripen properly, and a well-cultivated soil which has been well manured for a previous crop will produce the best plants.

Seed sowing

For the earliest crops I sow the seed in the greenhouse in late April or early May, maintaining a temperature of 13°C (55°F). The seeds are best sown 2·5 cm (1 in) deep in small peat pots of seed compost. After germination the seedlings should be gradually hardened off.

For sowings made from May onwards the seeds can be put directly into the ground where they are to grow. Insert them, 2·5 cm (1 in) deep, in groups of three leaving 38 cm (15 in) between the groups in the row and 1 m (3 ft) between the rows.

To produce cobs the female flowers have to be pollinated by pollen blown by the wind from the tassel-like male flowers at the tops

The cobs of sweet corn are ready for harvesting when the seeds exude a milky juice

of the plants, and this is best achieved if the plants are grown in square blocks rather than in a long, single row.

Planting

The greenhouse-raised plants should be planted out, at the spacing recommended for outdoor sowing, in late May.

Cultivation

Thin the outdoor-sown plants leaving one in each group as soon as they are large enough to single out. Hoe between the plants and water them regularly in dry weather.

Shake the plants now and then to assist pollination and apply a light dressing of general fertilizer in June, watering it in well. When the plants are 1 m (3 ft) high earth them up to a height of around 23 cm (9 in) to give some support.

Harvesting

The cobs are ready for harvesting as soon as the individual seeds

exude a milky juice when pierced with a knife or a finger nail; twist or cut the whole ear, which includes the sheath, as soon as it is ready. In dull, rainy seasons the yield will be reduced considerably.

Pests and diseases

It is unlikely that any pest or disease will give you much trouble with this crop.

Sweet corn plants should always be grown in a block to aid pollination

Tomatoes

Sow: March or early April under glass

Harvest: July to October

Tomatoes are, I think, an almost indispensable crop as the flavour of shop-bought ones bears no resemblance to that of the home grown.

Selected varieties. There is a range of varieties for growing both indoors and out. In my opinion the best for both purposes is Alicante, but Ailsa Craig and Moneymaker are both good, tried and tested varieties. The Amateur, Outdoor Girl, French Cross (bush) and Sugarplum are for outdoor use, and for something different there are yellow ones – Yellow Perfection – and the orange Tangella.

Outdoor cultivation

Seed sowing. Sow thinly in boxes in April and germinate in a temperature of 18°C (65°F). Prick out into pots and harden off in a cold frame.

Cultivation. Select the strongest short-jointed plants and set these out in early June 45 cm (1½ ft) apart in rows 75 cm (2½ ft) apart. The soil should contain plenty of well-rotted manure or compost and be dressed with general fertilizer at 85 g per square metre (3 oz per square yard) before planting. Choose a sunny sheltered position,

preferably facing south. Alternatively they can be grown in 25- or 30-cm (10- or 12-in) pots or peat bags on the patio, balcony or terrace. With the exception of the bush varieties, each plant should be kept to a single stem by removing the side shoots which grow in the angles formed by the leaf stalk and main stem. Provide each plant with a good stake and tie the growth to it at intervals.

Water well at planting time but then give rather less until the plants are well established and growing away. In dry weather plenty of water will be needed and a mulch around the roots will help to act as a sponge and contain what moisture there is.

Usually four or five trusses of fruits are sufficient for a plant to ripen out of doors and once these are formed the plant is stopped by pinching out the growing point. Feed weekly with a tomato fertilizer from the time the first fruits start to form.

Harvesting. The tomatoes should be picked as soon as they are well coloured. However, once there is danger of frost occurring it is advisable to cut off the trusses and bring them indoors to ripen – an airing cupboard is ideal. Alternatively, I untie the plants from their canes, lay them on straw on the ground and cover with cloches.

Bush varieties are allowed to grow without removing the side shoots. They then form branched plants which need little support. Apart from this they are grown as before.

Using peat bags is one of the simplest ways of growing tomatoes

Greenhouse cultivation

Seed sowing. I like to sow in Mid-March, although this can be done in February.

The method is as described under outdoor cultivation and the seedlings are pricked out into 9-cm (3½-in) pots and either gradually potted on into 23-cm (9-in) pots of John Innes potting compost No. 3 or planted in beds of well-prepared soil at a distance of 45 cm (1½ ft) apart.

Cultivation. Remove the side shoots as they form and support the main stems on canes or strings

De-side shooting tomatoes is a routine job which should not be neglected

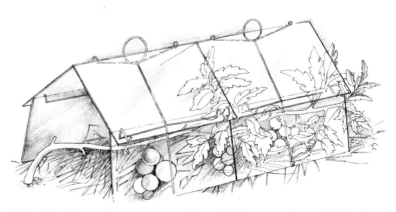

One method of ripening outdoor tomatoes at the end of the season is to untie the plant from its cane, lay it on straw on the ground and cover it with cloches

attached to wires stretched below the roof. Pinch out the growing points when the plants reach the glass. Water moderately at first and then more freely as growth increases.

From May onwards spray the plants with water to assist the flowers to set – I do this at midday if possible. Another important point is to ventilate freely in warm weather to prevent outbreaks of fungal disease.

Feed weekly with a proprietary tomato fertilizer once the fruits are set on the lowest truss. To obtain satisfactory crops try to maintain a minimum temperature throughout of 13°C (55°F).

Ring culture

I find this method of growing tomatoes very useful as only small amounts of soil are involved and so there is less risk of soil diseases developing.

The aim is to encourage two root systems – fine feeding roots which are confined to the compost (John Innes potting compost No. 3)

The variety Moneymaker can be relied upon to produce a good crop of tomatoes

When growing tomatoes by ring culture, water is applied only to the aggregate layer

in 23- or 25-cm (9- or 10-in) bottomless ring containers, and coarser roots which delve into a bed of some sterile aggregate (ashes, gravel) on which the containers are stood.

The plants are grown on to the final potting stage as previously described and are then potted into the special ring containers, which are stood on a 20-cm (8-in) deep layer of the aggregate. A first thorough watering is given through the rings but after this water is supplied to the aggregate only and this encourages the formation of the coarser root system. Once the first fruits are formed liquid feeds are applied weekly to the compost in the containers.

Apart from watering and feeding the plants are grown in the same way as before.

Pests and diseases

There are a number of diseases which may attack tomatoes – stem rot, potato blight, root rot, leaf mould, verticillium wilt and virus.

The pests are not quite so formidable but look out for wireworms, eelworm, whitefly and red spider. The last two are only likely to be a problem under glass.
See pages 70 to 73.

Other troubles. There are two disorders, known as blossom end rot and blotchy ripening, which result from bad cultivation, the first is due mainly to inadequate watering and the second to insufficient feeding.

Quick tip

Peat bags are a simple way of growing tomatoes both indoors and out. Although it is often recommended to allow three plants to each bag I prefer to grow two in a bag. The cultivation after planting is as described above. A bonus of this method of growing is that the peat provides good control of diseases such as wilt and soil pests such as eelworm and wireworm.

Turnip

Sow: February in frames and under cloches
March to September out of doors

Harvest: June onwards

Turnips are a useful vegetable for their long cropping period and their fresh, tangy flavour.

Selected varieties. For early crops I can do no better than recommend Snowball and Purple Milan, the first is round and the second flattish, and for both early and late sowings Golden Ball will give you round, golden roots which will last particularly well in store.

Soil preparation

If they are to produce crisp, tender roots, turnips must be grown quickly, so good supplies of both moisture and nutrients should be available in the soil. Ground which has been manured for a previous crop is ideal; as well as providing nutrition, the manure will also help to retain water.

Seed sowing

The seeds are sown in drills 1 cm ($\frac{1}{2}$ in) deep and 30 to 38 cm

As soon as turnips are a reasonable size lift and store them in boxes of sand

(12 to 15 in) apart and the seedlings are thinned to leave one every 15 to 23 cm (6 to 9 in).

The earliest crops are obtained by sowing in mid-February in cold frames or under cloches. Sowings from March onwards can be made in the open ground.

Cultivation

Apart from hoeing regularly between the rows and ensuring that adequate supplies of water are always available, the application of small dressings of a general fertilizer a couple of times through the growing season will be very beneficial. A rate of 25 g per square metre (1 oz per square yard) is sufficient.

Harvesting

For the most succulent turnips, pull the roots when they are quite young – about the size of a cricket ball. As the roots age their flavour will become stronger and the flesh slightly harder.

Storing. The later crops can be lifted all together in October.

Remove the tops and store the roots in boxes of dry peat or sand. This will save cold, wet journeys to the vegetable garden if you happen to need them in unfavourable weather.

Pests and diseases

Flea beetle is the most damaging pest along with turnip gall weevil. The main diseases which you are likely to have to contend with are mildew, soft rot and club root. See pages 70 to 73.

Other troubles. Loose soil or an excess of nitrogen in the soil may cause the plants to bolt.

Quick tip

The value of turnip tops should not be neglected and by sowing a hardy variety in September – Green Top White and Green Top Stone are ideal – you can produce a useful supply of spring greens. The tops are cut as they are needed.

Herbs

A selection of herbs grown in the garden will provide you not only with a very fragrant group of plants, but also with a store of different flavours which can be added to a wide variety of dishes.

Soil and situation

Do make sure that you grow herbs within easy reach of the kitchen – a small border or patch just outside the door is ideal, or even pots stood by the doorstep. If you have no garden at all, a window box will hold a small selection of your favourites.

Always pick a warm, sunny and sheltered spot and, if possible, a light, well-drained soil. If the soil is heavy or you are short of space, herbs can be grown in 15- to 20-cm (6- to 8-in) pots of John Innes potting compost No. 1. Do not give any fertilizers or liquid feed to the plants after they have been potted; they will only grow too strongly and their flavour may be affected.

Propagation

Annual kinds are always grown from seed which is sown either out of doors from March to May or under glass in March. For outdoor sowings the seed should be sown in drills 0·5 to 1 cm ($\frac{1}{4}$ to $\frac{1}{2}$ in) deep and the resulting seedlings thinned to a suitable spacing – this will depend on the ultimate size of the plants. Indoor sowings are made in pots or boxes and the seedlings are pricked out into boxes as soon as they are large enough to handle. Harden these seedlings off gradually and plant them out where required in mid- to late May.

The perennial herbs can be propagated either by cuttings or division. Rosemary, sage, winter savory and thyme are easily raised from cuttings 8 to 10 cm (3 to 4 in) long taken in August or September. The bottom cut should be made below a leaf joint, the

A herb garden can be both a useful and attractive garden feature. Pebbles and paving are a good complement to the herbs and make the task of picking easier in wet weather

lower leaves removed and the cuttings inserted in pots of John Innes seed compost. If kept through the winter in a cool greenhouse or frame they will be well rooted by the following spring and can be planted out individually in May.

The spreading types such as mint and chives are most easily propagated by division. Lift the clumps with a fork in autumn or spring and either split them up with your hands or with a knife – making sure that each division has sufficient roots and shoots. The new clumps are either replanted or given to friends.

Drying and storing

Herbs are picked fresh whenever possible but annual and herbaceous kinds can be dried for winter use. Cut suitable shoots on a warm, dry day around flowering time which is when the flavour is at its best. Take off any dead or damaged leaves and carefully tie the stems of each kind of herb into separate bunches. Hang up the bunches in a warm, dry place and as soon as the leaves are completely crisp rub them from the stems and store them in well-labelled, air-tight containers.

Try a few of the following herbs in

your garden. Mint, parsley and thyme are, perhaps, the most widely grown but why not experiment with some of the more unusual ones as well?

Basil, Sweet

Sweet basil is a half-hardy annual which can be sown either under glass in March or out of doors in mid-May. The plants will eventually grow to a height of 60 cm (2 ft) and they should have their tops pinched out when they are young to make them bushy. The leaves are particularly useful for flavouring tomato dishes but can also be used in green salads and with fish, meat and omelettes.

Chives

A kind of onion, chives form tight but spreading clumps of spiky leaves about 23 cm (9 in) high. Propagation is best carried out by dividing mature plants, but seed can be sown out of doors in March and the young plants thinned to leave one every 15 cm (6 in). Chives are perennial but the foliage dies down in winter and clumps should be lifted and divided as a matter of course every three or four years. It is a good idea to

Chives are equally useful for growing in the open ground or in a pot on the kitchen windowsill

Marjoram

The annual sweet marjoram is grown from seed sown under glass in March, and the perennial pot marjoram can be raised in the same way – though the seeds of this can also be sown out of doors in April and May and old plants can be divided. The first is about 60 cm (2 ft) high and the second up to 30 cm (12 in). Both can be used in a wide variety of dishes but are particularly good in soups and stews.

Mint

Mint is a valuable and widely grown herb but it can become a nuisance if it is not properly man-

It is a good idea to contain mint by planting the runners in a bottomless pail

pot up a clump each autumn and bring it indoors so that the leaves are retained for winter use. Chopped leaves are frequently used in cheese and egg dishes and can also be used to flavour soups, sauces and salads.

Fennel

Apart from the perennial fennel which is grown for its aniseed-flavoured seeds, stems and feathery leaves, there is also Florence fennel or finocchio, an annual which is grown for its swollen stem bases. Both are best grown from seed sown out of doors in late March.

Florence fennel

Thin the seedlings to a spacing of 38 cm (15 in) when they are large enough to handle – they will eventually grow into decorative plants 1·25 to 2 m (4 to 6 ft) high. Mature clumps can be divided but the resulting plants are usually slow in establishing themselves. Ordinary fennel is used to flavour fish, soups and salads, and the stem bases of Florence fennel are boiled and eaten as a vegetable.

Garlic

Garlic is an easily grown flavouring indispensable to many cooks. Each bulb is composed of many small 'cloves' and it is these which are planted, 5 cm (2 in) deep and 15 cm (6 in) apart, in rows 30 cm (12 in) apart in March. Cultivation is the same as for the onion and the bulbs are lifted and dried off in August. String the bulbs together and store them in a cool place. The crushed cloves are used in many dishes.

aged. It spreads by underground runners and to avoid these taking over the garden I suggest that you plant young divisions in a bottom-less bucket or oil drum sunk into the ground. Division is the best means of propagating mint and, wherever possible, it should be grown in moisture-retentive soil. Many kinds are available but the most commonly grown are the spearmint (*Mentha viridis*) and the apple mint (*M. rotundifolia*). Both these can be used to make sauces and jellies and to flavour a variety of dishes and drinks.

Parsley

Although it is a perennial, parsley is almost always treated as an annual and sown afresh each year. It prefers a rich, moist soil and it is here that seeds should be sown in early March, late May and August to give a year-round supply. The seedlings should be thinned to allow one every 23 cm (9 in). Remove the leaves, a few from each plant, as they are required and pinch out any flowering stems as they form. Parsley is an ideal subject for edging borders and growing in pots and is widely used both as an ingredient of sauces and as a garnish.

Rosemary

One of the larger herbs, rosemary will make an evergreen bush up to 1·5 m (5 ft) high. It is easily raised from cuttings taken in August or from seeds sown out of doors in April; one plant will be sufficient for most people's needs. Use the leaves to flavour meat, fish and cooked vegetables.

Sage

Sage is a useful herb and if grown in one of the coloured-leaved forms (which are of equal culinary value to the grey-leaved kind) it is a particularly decorative garden plant. It is a small evergreen shrub and can be propagated by cuttings in August or September; the ordinary variety can be grown from seed sown under glass in March. The plants will eventually grow to a height of 60 cm (2 ft) and will benefit from being clipped over after flowering to reduce their height by one half. Clumps should be lifted and divided every three or four years. Sage is extensively used in the preparation of stuffings.

Savory

There are two distinct kinds of savory – summer and winter – and both have a flavour which resembles that of sage. Summer savory is raised from seed sown out of doors in April, and winter savory either in the same way or from cuttings

taken in August and September. Both grow to a height of 30 to 45 cm (1 to 1½ ft). Summer savory is used to flavour meat, cooked vegetables, salads and stews and winter savory for stuffings, meat and fish.

Tarragon

This is a perennial herb growing to a height of 60 cm (2 ft) which needs some frost protection when it has died down in winter – sacking, ashes or bracken should be placed over the crowns. Propagation is by division in spring. Tarragon is

Salvia officinalis icterina is one of the interesting coloured forms of sage

used in flavouring soups and sauces and also in the preparation of tarragon vinegar.

Thyme

Thyme is an ideal subject for a sun-baked spot in the garden. It can be propagated by seed sown under glass in March or out of doors in April, by cuttings taken in May or June, or established plants can be divided in spring. The plants will grow to a height of 23 to 30 cm (9 to 12 in) and should be cut back to the ground or lifted and replanted every three years in spring. The leaves are used in stuffings and a wide variety of dishes.

Pests and Diseases of Vegetable Crops

Safety precautions

All chemicals should be applied strictly according to the manufacturer's instructions and protective clothing worn if recommended.

It is especially important to observe the periods of time which must be allowed to elapse between the applications of the insecticide and fungicide and the harvesting of the crops.

Keep all chemicals out of the reach of children and away from animals, and wash out all spraying apparatus after use.

Pest	Crops Attacked	Symptoms and Damage Caused	Control
Aphids (Greenfly and Blackfly)	A wide range, though blackfly is prominent on broad beans.	The aphids secrete honeydew which makes the plants sticky and encourages the growth of a fungus known as sooty mould. Leaves are distorted and the vigour of the plant is considerably reduced. Aphids also transmit virus diseases which, in their turn, can cripple the plant.	Spray with dimethoate, malathion or menazon. The tops of broad beans can be pinched out, after the first pods have formed, to discourage attack.
Asparagus beetle	Asparagus	Shoots and foliage are eaten by grey larvae. Bad attacks will reduce the foliage considerably.	Spray with gamma HCH*.
Cabbage caterpillars	Cabbages, cauliflowers, brussels sprouts and other brassicas	Leaves are eaten – only a skeleton is left after a bad attack.	Hand pick and destroy the caterpillars and yellow eggs wherever possible. Spray or dust the plants with derris, HCH* or malathion.
Cabbage root fly	Cabbages, cauliflowers, brussels sprouts and other brassicas	Wilting and blueing of the foliage coupled with stunted growth and often the death of the plant. If a plant is lifted and the roots are examined small, white grubs will be found tunnelling into the tap root. Smaller roots will have been completely eaten away.	Dust seedlings with 4% calomel dust when they are planted out. Repeat 2 weeks later. Dust seedbeds with gamma HCH* and dust around the stems after planting.
Cabbage whitefly	Cabbages and other brassicas	Sticky excrement is left on the leaves and the vigour of the crop is reduced.	Spray with gamma HCH* or malathion.
Carrot fly	Carrots and occasionally parsnips	Wilting and reddening of the leaves. If pulled, infected plants will be seen to have tunnels in their tap roots as a result of the burrowing of the small white larvae.	Dust the soil around the plants with naphthalene every 10 days after thinning until the end of June. Alternatively, dust between the young seedlings with gamma HCH*.
Celery fly (Celery leaf miner)	Celery	Whitish tunnels in the leaves. Attacks may be so bad as to remove all the green colouring from the leaves.	Pick off and burn any infected leaves if the attack is a mild one. Between May and August occasional sprays of malathion will keep this pest under control.
Cutworms	A wide range of crops	Wilting and loss of vigour, or the stems may be eaten away at ground level. If plants are pulled, the roots will be found to have been eaten away and the fat, greyish-cream caterpillars may be found in the soil.	Fork an insecticide containing gamma HCH* into the top few inches of the soil.
Earwigs	Various crops	Leaves and flowers are eaten.	Spray with gamma HCH*. Traps, in the form of plant pots filled with straw and placed upside down on top of canes, can be used to catch the insects. Empty these daily into a bucket of boiling water.
Eelworms	Onions, potatoes, tomatoes and other crops	Symptoms vary according to the crop attacked. All show a reduction in vigour and appear generally sick. Potatoes develop small white cysts on the roots and onions become swollen and misshapen.	Remove and burn any infected plants. Eelworms can survive in the soil for extremely long periods of time so crop rotation is advisable, keeping crops which have been attacked away from the site of infestation for as long as possible. Keep down weeds which may act as alternative hosts.

Pest	Crops Attacked	Symptoms and Damage Caused	Control
Flea beetle	Cabbages, cauliflowers and other brassicas, also radishes and turnips particularly in the seedling stage.	Small punctures, bleached areas and holes appear in the leaves.	Good cultivation and good soil will promote vigorous growth and give plants resistance to attack. Occasional dustings at the seedling stage with derris or gamma HCH* will discourage attack.
Mice	A wide range	Crops in store are frequently eaten, as are newly sown seeds – especially those of peas and beans.	Poisoned baits or traps can be used to protect stored vegetables. Poisoned baits should be used for crops in the open but be sure in both cases to prevent other animals or children from coming into contact with them by placing the bait under a tile.
Onion fly	Onions and leeks	Foliage turns yellow and wilts and if the bulbs are lifted they will be found to contain small, white maggots.	Remove and burn infected plants. Dust the soil with gamma HCH* at planting time and repeat the operation 2 weeks later. Dust the rows of seedlings with HCH* when the plants are 5 to 8 cm (2 to 3 in) high.
Pea and bean weevil	Pea and broad bean	Edges of the leaves are eaten giving the foliage a scalloped appearance.	Spray with gamma HCH* at the first signs of attack.
Pea moth	Pea	Maggots burrow into the pods and eat the peas.	Spray with carbaryl in the evening at flowering time.
Pigeons	Brassicas in particular, but also seedling peas	Leaves and seeds are eaten.	Fruit cages or netting placed over the vegetable garden in the autumn and left there until spring are the only really effective means of preventing damage.
Red spider mite	Various crops, particularly under glass and in hot, dry weather	Leaves become mottled with greyish spots and are eventually quite bleached, frequently falling prematurely.	Spray with derris, dimethoate or malathion. In greenhouses, fumigate with azobenzene and malathion.
Slugs	A wide range of crops	Leaves, stem bases and roots are eaten.	Slug bait, placed out of reach of children and animals (inside a small length of drainpipe or under a tile) will give good control.
Thrips	Mainly peas, but other kinds occasionally attack leeks and cucumbers	Sap is sucked and the damaged tissue has a silvery appearance.	Spray with dimethoate.
Turnip gall weevil	Turnips and other brassicas	Wilting of the plants. If a plant is pulled, the roots will be found to be considerably swollen and maggots will be seen to be present when the root is cut in half.	Carry out crop rotation. Burn infected roots. Ensure that the land is adequately supplied with nutrients to promote healthy growth. Infected soil can be dusted with gamma HCH*
Whitefly	Tomatoes and cucumbers; particularly those grown under glass	Leaves are coated with honeydew and the vigour of the plant is reduced.	Spray outdoor crops with malathion. Spray greenhouse-grown crops with malathion or fumigate with tetrachlorethane.
Wireworm	Potatoes, carrots and other root crops	Wilting and general weakening of the plant.	Treat seed with an organo-mercury dressing before sowing. Fork in naphthalene or dust soil with gamma HCH* if not occupied with crops. (Tainting will result if this is done when root crops are in the ground.)

*formerly BHC

Disease	Crops Attacked	Symptoms and Damage Caused	Control
Blossom end rot	Tomato	Blackened areas at the base of the fruits.	Apply sufficient water regularly to sustain the plant at all times. Erratic watering will encourage this physiological disorder.
Blotchy ripening	Tomato	Fruits blotched with hard areas which are green or yellow in colour.	Plant in adequately fertilized soil which is well drained yet moisture retentive. Shade the plants from bright sunshine. An application of sulphate of potash may effect a cure if it is well watered in.

Disease	Crops Attacked	Symptoms and Damage Caused	Control
Botrytis (grey mould)	A wide range of plants are attacked	Grey velvety growth and blackened tissue are evident on attacked stems, leaves and fruits. Plants may keel over and die as a result of rotting tissue.	Improve air circulation and cut down humidity. Gather outdoor crops before the weather becomes cold and wet. Spray with benomyl.
Brown heart	Turnips, but more especially swedes	Grey or brown areas in the centre of the root. Affected roots are inedible.	Ensure that a good supply of organic matter and nutrients are present in the soil. Grow resistant varieties.
Celery leaf spot	Celery	Brown spots appear on the leaves and eventually cause them to die.	This is a seed-borne disease and should not be encountered if the seed is purchased from a reputable merchant. Infected plants should be sprayed with Bordeaux mixture or zineb at fortnightly intervals until October.
Chocolate spot	Broad bean	Chocolate brown blotches on the leaves and brown streaks on the stems.	Spray with Bordeaux mixture or copper fungicide.
Club root	Brassicas	Wilting and blueing of the foliage. If infected plants are lifted they will be found to have swollen roots but these will not be infested by maggots as is the case with turnip gall weevil.	Acid soil should be limed to reduce the likelihood of attack. Dip the roots of seedlings in a paste of 4% calomel dust, or dust with calomel along the rows at planting time. Badly drained soils are especially liable to infection. Carry out crop rotation.
Crown rot	Rhubarb	The leaves become reddened, the stalks swollen and the crown brown and rotten.	Lift and burn infected plants. Do not replant on the same piece of ground if this can be avoided.
Damping off	A wide range of seedlings	Seedlings die as a result of fungal attack at the base of the stems which causes them to keel over.	Sow thinly and prick out as soon as possible. Watering with a solution of Cheshunt compound will reduce the likelihood of attack and prevent the disease spreading. Ventilate as freely as possible.
Mildew	A wide range of crops but particularly brassicas, spinach, peas, lettuce and onions	White, mealy deposits on the leaves which lead to a reduction in vigour and eventual browning of the foliage.	Spray with thiram or zineb.
Neck rot	Onions, particularly in store	Rotting of stem bases which become brown at first and then turn grey as mould develops.	Store only sound onions. The storing place should be dry and airy and the bulbs should be properly ripened and dried before they are brought in.
Parsnip canker	Parsnips	Brown or black patches on the roots. Entry can be gained through cracks in the roots caused by heavy applications of water after a dry period, through the tunnels made by carrot fly, and also through cracking due to an excess of organic matter in the soil.	Control carrot fly. Do not grow parsnips on heavily manured ground. Apply lime to ground where the disease has occurred before.
Potato blight	Potatoes and tomatoes	Moist brown or black patches on the leaves, rotting of stems and tubers (potatoes), and also fruits (tomatoes).	Spray foliage with Bordeaux mixture or zineb in early July and repeat at 2-week intervals until mid-September. Grow resistant varieties.
Potato scab	Potatoes	The tubers become covered in brown, flaky scabs. They are still edible.	Make sure that the land has adequate supplies of organic matter and dress limy soils with acid peat. Burn all infected potato peelings.
Potato wart disease	Potatoes	Warty outgrowths on the stem bases and tubers. Flesh may rot completely.	This is a serious disease and the Ministry of Agriculture should be notified of its presence. Whenever possible grow varieties which are immune to the disease.
Root rot	Tomatoes under glass	Wilting of the plants starts at the top and works its way down.	Water the plants carefully and give them a well-drained soil, and an adequate temperature. To control the disease in affected plants, give a topdressing of moist peat, adequate shade from bright sunshine and an occasional overhead spray with tepid water.

Disease	Crops Attacked	Symptoms and Damage Caused	Control
Soft rot	Various crops, including those in store	Softening and decay of central tissue in roots and stems. Roots eventually turn grey and slimy and usually smell unpleasant.	Grow the plants in soil containing a good supply of nutrients. Keep down pests which could allow entry of the disease. Store only healthy roots.
Stem rot (Foot rot)	Cucumbers, melons and tomatoes	Rotting of the stems just above soil level, and eventual collapse of the plant.	Plant on small mounds of well-drained compost and grow the plants in sufficiently high temperatures. Dust around infected plants with captan. Avoid splashing water on to the fruits. Ensure that seed leaves are well above the soil when planting.
Tomato leaf mould	Tomato	Pale yellow spots on the leaves, leading to eventual withering of the foliage.	Ventilate greenhouses adequately and remove and burn infected leaves. Spray infected plants with zineb or benomyl.
Verticillium wilt	Tomato	Wilting and yellowing of the leaves, starting at the bottom of the plant.	Keep greenhouses shaded and warm and spray the foliage occasionally with tepid water. Remove and burn badly infected plants and treat infected soil with Cheshunt compound. In bad cases, the soil should be replaced.
Virus disease	Many crops	Mottling, distortion, stunted growth, death of tissue.	Remove and burn any infected plants. Keep down aphids and other insects which can transmit these diseases.
White rot	Onion	Leaves turn yellow and wilt. Roots rot completely away. Bulbs are covered in white fungus.	Remove and burn infected plants. Dust seed drills with 4% calomel dust at sowing time.

Growing Fruit

It is becoming more and more popular to grow fruit of one kind or another and even the smallest of gardens can grow some. And for people without a garden a fruit tree in a tub or pot makes a useful and ornamental feature for a paved area or conservatory.

The fruits grown in this country are divided into two main groups: the soft fruit and the top or tree fruit. The first group includes the red, white and black currants, and the various berries, while the second group is made up of all the fruits which grow on some sort of tree – apples, pears, cherries, etc.

When deciding where to plant fruit you should bear in mind their general requirements of a sunny, sheltered position and a fairly good soil with a depth of at least 30 cm (12 in).

What fruit to grow

The decision of which fruit to grow rests on two factors – the first the family's likes and dislikes, and the second the area available. I don't think I need say anything about the first, after all this will be a personal decision, but on the question of what space is available and how best it can be filled there are certain considerations which must be taken into account.

If it is at all possible the best solution is to set aside an area of the garden for growing fruit only. This means that the growing regime and spraying programme can go on uninterrupted by the presence of other plants. Grouping the fruit together will also allow you to put up some permanent form of protection against the birds, such as a fruit cage – this is really the only way of dealing successfully with this particular problem.

In areas devoted to fruit I like to see the different fruits kept together and planted in rows. It might be helpful to remember in planning the planting that apples, red currants and gooseberries have similar feeding needs and require a lot of potash, whereas pears, black currants, and plums need more nitrogen.

Obviously just how much fruit can be fitted in will depend on the space but I would suggest concentrating first on a range of dessert and culinary apples grown as cordons – apples are particularly good value both for their long cropping season and good keeping qualities. I would grow pears as well although in smaller quantities as they are not so useful as apples for storing. Raspberries are the best value of the soft fruit, followed by black currants.

Larger areas can, of course, accommodate a wider range of fruit. I would only grow peaches, nectarines, apricots and cherries where suitable wall space is available. Strawberries are not long term and can often be grown in the vegetable garden or even in pots or barrels.

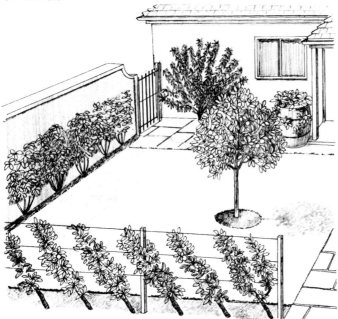

Make use of any available wall space and grow fruit also as decorative trees and screens

Where there is not sufficient space to set aside a separate area for the fruit then the first decision must be which fruit to grow and I think that the soft fruits are the ones most easily accommodated and most generally useful. Of these my first choice would always be raspberries with their long cropping season and excellence as a frozen fruit, then come black currants, strawberries and gooseberries. There are, however, various ways of finding room for other fruit. Consider, for instance, growing blackberries and loganberries against a wall or fence – not necessarily a sunny one – then the house or garage walls may provide a home for fan-trained peaches or nectarines if they are south or south-west facing, or plums and acid cherries such as Morello if they are north or east facing. Cordon apples and pears may also be grown against a wall or, and this is how I use them, as an ornamental screen between various parts of the garden.

The importance of rootstocks

Most of the top fruit, apples, pears, plums, etc., cannot be grown successfully from pips or stones because they do not come true to variety. Commercially, therefore, each variety is propagated by budding or grafting it or to what is known as a rootstock. The type of rootstock used influences both the size to which the tree will grow and the time when it will start producing fruit. For example, an apple budded or grafted onto a dwarfing rootstock will always be relatively dwarf growing and will start bearing fruit some two years after budding, whereas one grown on a stronger-growing rootstock will grow taller and will be longer coming into bearing.

The important point about these rootstocks is that all the rootstocks of one type are exactly the same and will affect the grafted variety in the same way giving a uniformity of vigour and performance. For a small garden, therefore, and for trees which are to be grown as cordons and dwarf pyramids it is important to buy them grafted or budded onto dwarfing or semi-dwarfing rootstocks. The bud or shoot grafted onto the stock is known as the scion.

Pollination

Another point to remember when choosing your top fruit is to buy varieties which are either self-fertile or will pollinate each other. Failure to do this may mean that you will get no fruit setting.

Pollination is the term used to describe the transference of pollen from the male to female parts of the flower and it is particularly important in the case of fruit trees if they are to bear good crops. Many plants are self-fertile and can pollinate themselves but others, including a lot of the tree fruits, are self-sterile and require cross pollination. In the case of fruit this means that the pollen must be carried from one variety to another of the same kind of fruit. More details of this are given where necessary under the individual fruits. Apples, pears, plums and cherries are the fruits

The soft fruits give a good return on the space they occupy as they crop well and are useful for preserving

loganberries and the currants – will crop well in a certain amount of shade but this is not true of the majority.

Shelter from wind and weather is necessary because many of the fruits flower early and can be badly affected by frost, indeed to such an extent that the flowers and buds may be killed. Hedges and fences are the most effective forms of protection as they cut the force of the wind but still allow some air to filter through, and this movement of air prevents the build-up of cold air in the lee of the screen and in turn means that there is less likelihood of frost damage. Walls, unless very tall, only protect those plants growing immediately in their lee.

The ideal soil is one which is deep, well drained and moisture retentive. Fruit can, however, be grown on a wide range of soils if attention is paid to the initial preparation and subsequent feeding and management. As fruit crops will occupy the same piece of ground for a long time, the soil must be prepared by digging it as deeply as possible, at the same time removing all perennial weeds and working in a good quantity of well-rotted organic matter. About 10 days before planting give a dressing of general fertilizer.

The remarks concerning the preparation of soil for vegetable growing (see page 14) all apply to fruit crops and you should again carry out a soil test to check the acidity. Applications of hydrated lime may be required if the soil is very acid but fruit, unlike vegetables, does best on a slightly acid soil.

mostly affected by self-sterility; most of the soft fruits are self-fertile.

Where fruit trees in adjoining gardens are comparatively close this may be sufficient for cross pollination to be carried out, provided, of course, that they are in flower at the same time. But this is rather a hit-and-miss affair and I do recommend that you plant your own pollinators if possible.

Soil and situation

Fruit grows best in an open position but protection from the wind is essential; some kinds – blackberries,

Planting

November to March is the usual time for planting trees, bushes and canes which have been lifted from the open ground. Container-grown trees can be planted at any time as long as they are watered well first, planted not too deeply, and watered again if the weather is dry. If container-grown plants are bought in flower or fruit then this should be left on because as the roots have not suffered too much disturbance the trees can be allowed to bear fruit straightaway.

Planting a tree The tree is placed in position and the roots are spread out

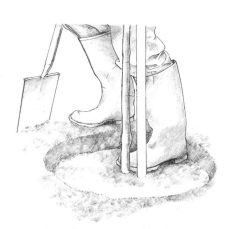

Return the soil in layers, working it in between the roots and firming it well

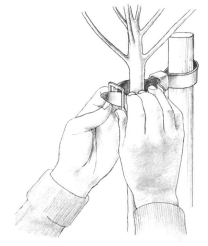

The trees must be securely staked and tied to give them stability

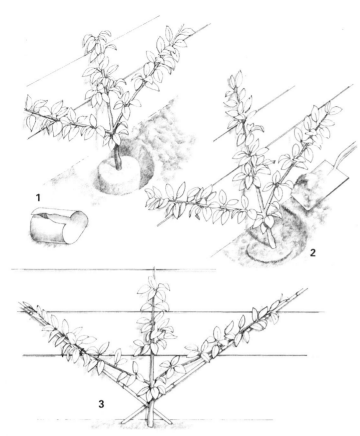

Planting a wall-trained container-grown tree 1. Make a hole large enough to hold the root ball and remove the tree from its container, taking care not to disturb the roots. **2.** Place the tree in the hole. **3.** After returning the soil and firming it, support the branches with canes

However, I prefer to order my trees for November planting as I find they suffer less of a check by being transplanted when they are completely dormant.

What age of tree is it best to buy? The one-year-old or maiden tree is the cheapest and also the easiest to establish but you have the problem of training it to whatever form you want and you will have to wait longer for it to fruit. Two- or three-year-old partially trained trees should produce fruit two years after planting; they may well carry their first fruit in one year but these should be taken off in fairness to the tree.

By the way, if the trees arrive from the nursery during a spell of frosty weather it is better to keep them in their wrappings in a frost-free place for a few days rather than to risk planting them. In the event of the bad weather persisting then 'heel in' the trees for a spell; do this by laying the trees down at an angle with their roots in a trench, and then cover the roots with soil and firm it in well around them.

The actual planting procedure is important, and I start by making a hole which is wide enough to allow the roots to be fully spread out. I then put in a stake and position the tree, spreading its roots and

trimming off any damaged ones. Do not plant too deeply – take as a guide the old soil mark on the stem which shows the depth at which the plant was growing in the nursery. The union between rootstock and scion must be kept above soil level to prevent the scion throwing out roots. When returning the soil, work it carefully in between the roots and replace it in layers, firming each well. Finally place a firm tie between the tree and stake to prevent wind rock. Planting distances are given under the individual fruits.

Wall-trained trees. Fruit to be grown as wall-trained specimens is planted in the same way but, because the soil against the wall is usually rather dry, the planting holes are dug some 30 cm (12 in) away from the wall and the main stem is inclined backwards. A single stake is not required, the branches are tied to bamboo canes as they develop and these in turn are tied to the supporting wires.

Walls to be used for growing fruit should be at least 2·25 m (7 ft) high, and 3 to 3·5 m (10 to 12 ft) is a better proposition. Vine eyes are used to support the wires 8 to 10 cm (3 to 4 in) away from the wall, and the wires are stretched tautly at 30-cm (12-in) intervals from the bottom to the top of the wall.

Cordon trees. Apples and pears to be trained as cordons are usually grown obliquely. These should be planted at an angle of 45 degrees making sure that the scion part of the union between rootstock and scion is uppermost. The easiest way of planting cordons is to make a trench rather than individual holes.

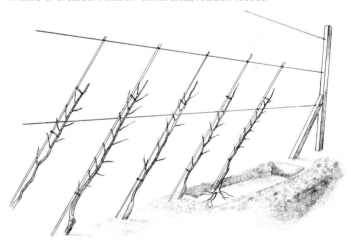

Cordons are planted in a trench with their stems inclined at an angle of 45 degrees

Red and white currants and gooseberries can also be grown as cordons and can either be planted obliquely or upright.

Whichever method of training is adopted the supporting wires must be strong and securely attached to metal or wooden posts set at 3·5-m (12-ft) intervals, or they can be secured to walls or fences. The bottom wire is set at a height of about 75 cm (2½ ft) above the level of the soil and the other two (three is the usual number) at intervals of 60 cm (2 ft). As with wall-trained trees the stems are supported by canes which are tied to the wires.

General cultivation

Mulching

This is a very necessary part of the growing regime for fruit as it helps to improve the moisture-holding capacity of the soil and keeps the roots cool. A range of materials can be used as a mulch, well-rotted farmyard manure and garden compost, straw, peat, composted tree bark or black polythene.

The mulch is spread around the trees or bushes in a layer 8 to 10 cm (3 to 4 in) thick and over an area covered by the extent of the branches, but it should not be allowed to touch the main stems. I always give a dressing of a general fertilizer first and then apply the mulch in spring or early summer when the soil has had a chance to warm up.

All fruit trees benefit from a mulch applied in late spring

Feeding

All fruits need an adequate supply of inorganic or non-bulky organic fertilizers to give them the nutrients they require. I have already mentioned the plant's need for certain chemicals on page 14, and will just add that for the tree fruit I always use a rose fertilizer at a rate of 110 to 225 g per square metre (4 to 8 oz per square yard) in February or March. Other individual feeding requirements are mentioned under each fruit.

Watering

Fruit makes a heavy demand on water in the spring and early summer and as these seasons are, more often than not, dry, water conservation is most important. In building up the moisture-retentiveness of the soil you can have no better aid than organic matter dug in before planting and then used as the annual mulch.

Protection

One of the major problems with fruit is protecting it from the birds – not only do the buds come under

Cordon pears grown in a fruit cage for protection

attack but also the developing fruits. I have found that birds get used to most forms of bird scarers and the only effective measure is the use of a fruit cage. Small areas of fruit or individual bushes can be protected by draping string or plastic netting over the branches.

Grassing down

The grassing down of fruit trees is often a matter for some discussion. I think that it is undoubtedly best for the trees to keep a cultivated area some 45 cm (18 in) around the stems for the first few years until they have become established. These areas can be kept weed and grass free by the use of herbicides such as paraquat.

If the grass is allowed to grow up to the stems then you must do more feeding to counteract the extra nitrogen taken up by the grass.

Weed control

If the area around the fruit trees or bushes is not put down to grass then it must be kept free from weeds. Many fruits are shallow rooting so any hoeing must be done with care. However, there are a number of herbicides which will do the job most effectively.

Pest and disease control

There are a great many pests and diseases which can attack fruit but fortunately only a few actually do so and it is not necessary to take precautions against them all. The most important thing to remember is that trees which are growing well are less likely to be attacked or will not be so badly damaged if they are, so general cultivation must not be neglected. Keep a look out for trouble, however, and take action quickly, in fact I usually follow a routine spray pro-gramme for apples and pears (see page 87) each year which takes care of most of the usual pests and diseases.

A table of pests and diseases of fruit together with suggested control measures is given on pages 120 to 123.

Non-production of fruit

The following six rules sum up the most important aspects of cultivation and if one or more of them is lacking then it may well lead to no fruit being produced.

1. Provide shelter from frost and cold winds.
2. Make sure that where necessary suitable pollinators are grown.
3. Try to give some protection from birds.
4. In very fertile soil some trees will put on a lot of vegetative growth at the expense of fruit buds. To counteract this tie the shoots down in a curve to encourage the production of fruit buds.
5. Take care with pruning, wrong pruning and too much pruning can result in poor fruit production.
6. Feed the trees annually.

Fruit growing in containers

If space in the garden is in short supply or you would like something a bit different for the patio, terrace, conservatory or sun lounge, why not grow a fruit tree in a pot?

When I was a journeyman gardener at Windsor Castle I was put in charge of the orchard house where all the trees were grown in what we then called bushel pots. These were some 15 in to $1\frac{1}{2}$ ft in diameter and the same in depth and in them we grew peaches, nectarines, cherries, plums, figs, apples, and pears. The trees were watered every day and fed regularly with liquid fertilizer. Every second year they were taken out of their pots and as much of the soil as possible was teased out from between the roots with a pointed stick. The trees were then replaced in the same pots and new compost worked in around the sides and among the roots. The fruit, especially the cherries, was some of the best I ever tasted.

Growing trees in pots either indoors or out has several advantages. First, they come into cropping more quickly, in fact if potted up in the autumn they will often carry fruit in the following year if they are growing on a dwarfing rootstock. Then those which are kept out of doors are much easier to protect against frost damage in the earlier part of the year by covering them with netting or keeping them in the shelter of the house wall. Later on they can also be easily netted to keep the birds away from the buds and the fruit.

When selecting the varieties try to choose self-fertile ones. With cherries and pears this is impossible so it will be necessary to grow at least two trees of each, choosing compatible varieties.

The type of tree I would recommend for growing in containers is the bush on a dwarfing rootstock and

Fruit trees can be grown in containers to make decorative features for the patio or conservatory

either a maiden or two-year-old tree should be planted.

A good tree can be grown in a 25- to 30-cm (10- to 12-in) pot or a 30- to 45-cm (12- to 18-in) container with a minimum depth of 25 cm (10 in). Drainage holes in the base are essential and I always add some crocks, gravel or clinker ash to assist the drainage. For compost use John Innes potting compost No. 3. Soak the roots of the trees before planting and when potting ram the soil really firmly in, taking care to leave enough space between the top of the compost and the rim of the pot to allow for sufficient water to be applied to soak the compost right through. Water thoroughly throughout the year and feed once the plants are established; I prefer to use a tomato fertilizer for this and to give it once a week in spring, summer and into autumn. The trees should be re-moved from their pots every other year and the soil changed as I have already described.

The size of the tree depends to some extent on the feeding and watering, but the roots are restricted and so this restricts the height. Pruning should not be overdone and I rely mostly on summer pruning, cut-ting out diseased or overcrowded branches at other times of the year if necessary.

Recommended varieties for growing in containers

Apples. Discovery, Worcester Pearmain, Ellison's Orange and Laxton's Superb are dessert kinds, and for cooking Lord Derby, Lane's Prince Albert and Rev. W. Wilks.

Pears. Conference and Williams' Bon Chrétien.

Peaches and Nectarines. Peregrine (peach), Pine Apple and Early Rivers (nectarine).

Plums. Victoria is a good general purpose one, also Oullin's Golden Gage, Golden Transparent, Dennis-ton's Superb or Early Transparent Gage.

Cherries. Black Heart or Elton Heart.

Apples

Even with a limited amount of space it is worth thinking in terms of growing a range of apple varieties to cover the longest possible season of cropping as well as providing for both dessert and culinary needs.

Selected varieties

These are some of the favourite varieties listed with their time of cropping.

Dessert apples – early: Beauty of Bath and Scarlet Pimpernel; mid-season: Ellison's Orange, Worcester Pearmain, Winston, Sunset, Crispin, Cox's Orange Pippin (not a good variety for the northern parts of Britain), Egremont Russet if your tastes run to a russet apple, and another apple I like very much is Ribston Pippin, in fact, I prefer it to Cox; late: Laxton's Superb, Crawley Beauty.

Culinary apples – early: Early Victoria (also called Emneth Early); mid-season: Charles Ross, Rev. W. Wilks; late: Lane's Prince Albert (the best all-round cooker for the average size garden), Newton Wonder, Bramley's Seedling, Annie Elizabeth, and Blenheim Orange, which is a good dual-purpose variety.

Pollination

Apples exhibit a certain amount of self-sterility some being completely self-sterile, others partially so, but all crop better if cross pollination is allowed for by planting more than one variety. However, the varieties chosen must be ones that come into flower at the same time, and in the table I have suggested suitable pollinators for some of the most popular varieties.

There is an added complication in that certain varieties, e.g. Bramley's Seedling, are what is called triploid (carrying three times the usual number of chromosomes) and are bad pollinators and so cannot be used for this purpose. This means that if one of these varieties is

A tree trained on an espalier makes a decorative and useful screen

planted then at least three varieties must be grown – one to pollinate the Bramley's Seedling and another to pollinate the pollinator!

In a small garden cross pollination is, perhaps, most easily allowed for by planting a row of cordons and mixing up the varieties within the row.

Rootstocks

Once you have made the important decision of which variety you wish to grow you must then decide on the most appropriate rootstock to suit your particular needs, this will depend on the size of the garden, type of soil and the form which the tree is to take.

The range of rootstocks now available has been numbered to help identification. The differences between them lie in their vigour or otherwise and the speed with which they bring the budded or grafted variety into cropping.

For most purposes nowadays I would recommend one of the following types.

M.9 (Malling 9). This is the most dwarfing of the rootstocks and particularly good for small gardens,

Apple varieties can be divided into groups according to their season of flowering. Varieties occurring within the same groups will pollinate each other.

Early	Beauty of Bath, Egremont Russet, Laxton's Fortune, Lord Lambourne, Rev. W. Wilks, Ribston Pippin (T), Scarlet Pimpernel
Mid-season	Annie Elizabeth, Blenheim Orange, Bramley's Seedling (T), Charles Ross, Cox's Orange Pippin, Crispin (T), Early Victoria, Ellison's Orange, Golden Delicious, James Grieve, Lane's Prince Albert, Laxton's Superb, Newton Wonder, Sunset, Tydeman's Late Orange, Winston, Worcester Pearmain
Late	Crawley Beauty, Edward VII, Heusgen's Golden Reinette

T = Triploid varieties, not good pollinators

especially as it can be used for most varieties and also for bush, cordon, and espalier trees. Varieties grown on this stock should come into bearing in two or three years.

However, it is a stock for use on good, well-drained soil and is not recommended for sandy, gravelly or heavy clay soils which are lacking in organic matter.

M.26 (Malling 26). This produces a slightly bigger tree which does not crop so quickly or so heavily as M.9 but it is a better stock to choose if you have only average to poor soil. A good stock for bushes, cordons, espalier trained and dwarf pyramids.

MM.106 (Malling-Merton 106). This is a semi-dwarfing stock which is stronger than the previous two and produces both earlier and heavier crops. A better choice than M.9. for poor soil. It can be used for the same range of trees as M.26.

M.7 (Malling 7). This is similar to MM.106 and is used in the same way.

M.2 or MM.111. These two stocks bring trees into bearing later. They make larger trees on good soil but only medium-sized ones on poor soil. They are useful for large espaliers and half and full standards.

I cannot stress too much the importance of choosing the correct rootstock for your apple trees, after all they are likely to be with you for a long time. When you have decided which you want go to a reputable nurseryman, and don't be put off if the one you want is not available, with crops as long term as this I always think that it is better to wait another year rather than plant something which is not quite right. And extra time spent cultivating the soil and digging in organic matter will not be wasted.

Soil and situation

By and large there is an apple variety to suit most soils, although on poor or sandy soil the fruits may be smaller and not of such good quality. Without doubt, though, the best soil is one that is deep with good drainage. As these are very long-term crops it is important that the preparation is done properly and plenty of well-rotted garden compost or manure is dug in as deeply as possible. Heavy water-logged soils will lead to the development of canker on some varieties and root rotting.

Forms of trees

Apples can be trained in a number of ways to fit in with the size and needs of the garden. Standards and half-standards take up too much space for many modern gardens and they have been largely superseded by the bush and dwarf pyramids, or one of the trained forms – cordons and espalier.

Bush. This has a stem of 60 to 90 cm (2 to 3 ft) and a goblet-shaped head of branches arising from almost the same point.

Dwarf pyramids. The main stem is about 30 cm (12 in) long and the branches arise at intervals and decrease in length the higher up the tree they arise.

Cordon. The simplest form consists of a single stem trained at an angle of 45 degrees with the side growths pruned back to encourage the production of fruiting spurs. There are double and triple forms.

Espalier. Here we have a central stem with pairs of branches trained at right angles from it.

Half-standards. Similar to a bush but with a main stem of 1·25 to 1·5 m (4 to 5 ft).

Standard. Once again this is similar to a bush but in this case the main stem is 1·5 to 2 m (5 to 6 ft). This must be grown on a vigorous rootstock.

Planting

The planting of trees is described on page 77.

The planting distances for the various types of tree are as follows:

Forms of trees 1. Half-standard. **2.** Bush. **3.** Dwarf pyramid. **4.** Cordon. **5.** Espalier-trained

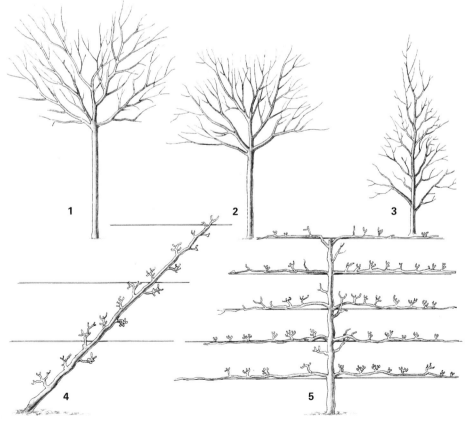

Bush on M.9 – 2·5 to 3 m (8 to 10 ft).
M.26 – 3 to 4·5 m (10 to 15 ft).
M.7 and MM.106 – 3·5 to 5·5 m
(12 to 18 ft).

Cordon on M.9 and M.26 – 75 cm
to 1 m (2½ to 3 ft) apart in the
rows, with 2 m (6 ft) between the
rows.

Espalier on M.9 (only suitable for
small trees) – 3 m (10 ft).
M.26 – 3 to 3·5 m (10 to 12 ft).
M.7 and MM.106 – 3·5 to 4·5 m
(12 to 15 ft).
M.2 and M.111 for large espaliers –
4·5 to 5·5 m (15 to 18 ft).

Dwarf pyramid on M.26, M.7
and MM.106 – plant 1 m (3 ft)
apart in the rows and space the
rows 2·25 m (7 ft) apart.

Standards on vigorous rootstocks –
6 to 8 m (20 to 25 ft).

Pruning

There are two main objectives in
pruning, the first to form a balanced
tree and the second to regulate the
formation of fruit buds.

Winter pruning is usually done
between leaf fall and bud burst and
you should remember that the
harder you prune the more strongly
the tree will grow and in young
trees this delays cropping.

Summer pruning is used mainly
for the restricted forms – dwarf
pyramids, cordons and espalier and
it consists of pruning back the lateral
shoots in July and August to four
or five leaves from the basal
cluster.

A one-year-old tree is known as a
maiden and while these are the
cheapest to buy they will take longer
to come into fruiting than a two- or
three-year-old tree and require
more training in the initial stages.

Bush. The pruning procedure for
the first two years starting with a
maiden tree is shown in the illustration.
Third year onwards. Shorten
the leaders by about a third and cut

It is important to recognize the different
sorts of buds and shoots if subsequent
pruning is to be done effectively

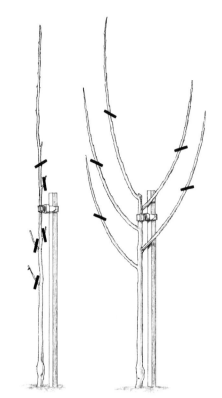

Pruning a bush tree *Left* In the winter
after planting cut the main stem back to
75 cm (30 in). *Right* In the second winter
retain four or five side shoots to form leaders
and shorten these by a half, making the cuts
to outward-pointing buds

the laterals to within two or three
buds of the main stems. The
shortening of the laterals will encourage the formation of fruiting
buds and spurs.

Spurs are short shoots which
carry clusters of fruit buds. Fruit
buds can be distinguished from the
other type of bud – growth buds –
by the fact that they are plump
whereas the growth buds are
narrow and pointed.

Once the tree is well established,
from the third or fourth year, little
pruning is required – remove badly
placed or damaged branches and
excess spurs.

Tip bearing. An added complication arises with certain varieties
which are known as tip bearers
because of their habit of producing
their fruit buds towards the tips of
the shoots. Bramley's Seedling and
Worcester Pearmain are two well-
known examples. With these it is
necessary to leave a good number
of the lateral shoots unpruned
otherwise you will simply be cutting away all the fruiting wood.

Dwarf pyramid. No pruning is
carried out when the maiden tree
is planted but when the buds start
to grow the main stem is cut back
to about 50 cm (20 in) and any side
growths over 15 cm (6 in) shortened
to five buds.

During the next winter, cut the
leader back to leave about 20 cm
(8 in) of new growth and make the
cut to a bud going in the opposite
direction to the one chosen for the
previous cut. The laterals should
be cut back to 13 to 15 cm (5 to
6 in) and an outward pointing bud.

The central leader is pruned in
this way each year until the tree
reaches a height of 2·25 m (7 ft).
The leader can then be cut back
into the old wood at blossom time.
This restricts growth.

Every summer the leaders, other
than the central one, should be
cut back to five or six leaves from
the basal cluster. At the same time
the laterals should be cut back to
three leaves and the sub-laterals to
one leaf.

Continue to prune in this manner,

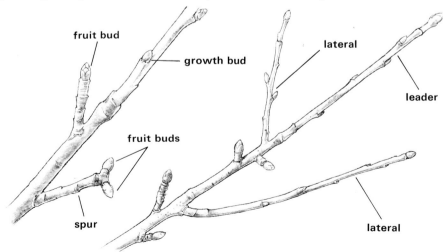

84

if necessary cutting out any excess spurs or badly placed branches during the winter.

Cordons. These require only summer pruning to restrict the growth of laterals. The leading shoot is left untouched unless there are not enough laterals when it can be shortened in winter by up to one-third of its length. When the cordon reaches the top of the support it can be lowered by 10 degrees or more.

If the leader does need pruning it should be done in May.

Espaliers. With this type of tree it is better to plant two- or three-year-old trees which have had the tricky initial training done. Maidens should be treated as shown in the accompanying illustrations.

This treatment should be repeated until the desired number of side arms have been produced. When this happens only two shoots are allowed to grow from the leader and these are trained in opposite directions to form the final pair of arms.

Fruit thinning

Apple trees left to carry too heavy a crop usually produce rather poor quality, small fruit, and in addition it may encourage them to

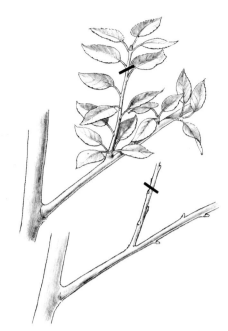

Summer pruning In summer pinch back the laterals to five or six leaves. Shorten these to two or three buds in winter

become biennial bearers – carrying a heavy crop every other year with little fruit in between. There is a natural drop of fruitlets, known as the June drop, in early July, but this may not be sufficient on its own and then I usually carry out some additional thinning. This is done when the fruitlets are about the size of golf balls and I make a point of removing the 'king' fruit (the one at the centre of the cluster) first and then any badly shaped fruits. Aim to leave one or two fruits on each truss.

Above **Pruning a dwarf pyramid 1.** When the tree is planted cut the stem back to 50 cm (20 in). **2.** In the following year cut the central leader back to leave 20 cm (8 in) of new growth, and shorten the laterals. **3.** In succeeding summers shorten the side growths and laterals as shown

Right **Pruning an espalier-trained tree 1.** In the winter after planting cut the main stem to a bud above the first wire. Try to select a bud which has two good buds close together beneath it. **2.** Train the resulting shoots as shown and gradually lower the side branches to the horizontal position. **3.** Repeat the pruning procedure of the first year in the second and subsequent winters until the required number of side arms has been produced

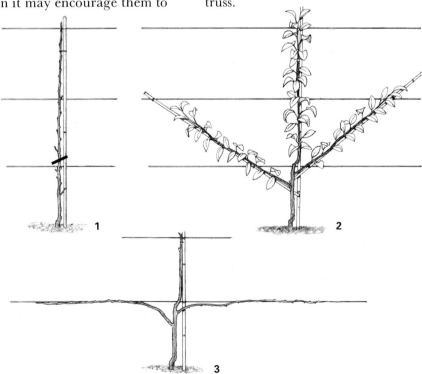

Feeding

Apples require a good supply of potash but it needs to be properly balanced with nitrogen; a suitable dressing to apply in February or March is 25 g (1 oz) of sulphate of ammonia plus 25 g (1 oz) of sulphate of potash to the square metre (square yard). I prefer to use a rose fertilizer and apply this at 110 to 225 g per square metre (4 to 8 oz per square yard).

Harvesting and storing

When it comes to picking time it is important to handle the fruit with care, especially if you intend to store it.

The best way of deciding if the fruit is ripe is to lift it and twist slightly – a mature apple will part readily from the branch. While early varieties are better picked slightly unripe, the late-keeping kinds should be left on the tree as long as conditions – and birds – allow.

When thinking in terms of storing apples, only late-maturing ones will keep for any length of time. The early season are not stored and the mid-season will only keep for a short time.

Choose only sound fruit for storing and I find that the best method is to wrap each fruit in waxed or tissue paper and then put them in single layers in slatted wooden boxes (tomato boxes with high corners are ideal) which can be stacked on top of each other and then placed in a dry, cool but frostproof place.

Look the fruit over at intervals to see if there are any signs of brown rot and remove any affected by it.

Apples will freeze, either sliced or as a purée.

Pests and diseases

Apples are very susceptible to attack from a number of pests and diseases and I think that it is almost impossible to grow a crop that is palatable and undamaged without making use of a certain amount of insecticide and fungicide.

Mid- and late-season apples can be wrapped in waxed paper and stored in boxes. Check through them at intervals and remove any which show signs of rotting

The caterpillars of the codling moth and apple sawfly give us maggoty apples, while aphids may heavily infest the young shoots and leaves. Winter moth caterpillars, apple sucker, apple blossom weevil, mussel scale, tortrix moth caterpillars, capsid bugs and fruit tree red spider mite all add to the problem.

On the disease front canker, scab, powdery mildew and brown rot may be seen. See pages 120 to 123.

In order to have good control you must time the application of sprays accurately and I have given here a simple spraying programme which will take care of most of the troubles.

I cannot stress too much the importance of reading the manufacturer's instructions with regard to the application of chemicals. Do not spray when the blossoms are fully open or at other times when the bees are active.

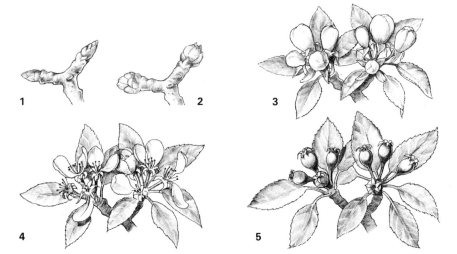

The various stages of apple (and pear) blossom are important guidelines for timing the application of protective sprays. **1.** Dormant. **2.** Bud burst. **3.** Pink bud (white bud in pears). **4.** Petal fall. **5.** Fruitlet

Time of Application	Insecticide or Fungicide	Pest or Disease
November to February	Tar oil winter wash	Eggs of overwintering insects, lichen and moss
Bud burst	HCH	All insect pests
Fortnightly to petal fall avoiding open blossom	HCH and captan	Insect pests and scab
After petal fall	Karathane and captan	Scab, apple mildew, red spider mite

The sprays applied up to the fruitlet stage are the most effective.

Other troubles

Bitter pit may be seen on the fruits. This is recognized as small brown spots occurring beneath the skin and throughout the flesh. Although the cause is not known for sure it seems to have something to do with water shortage, so mulching and watering during dry spells will help.

Bitter pit may also occur in fruit from trees which have been heavily pruned, and to reduce such occurrences the best course of action is to prune more lightly and to dress the soil with sulphate of potash at 110 g to the square metre (4 oz to the square yard).

Fruit cracking. This also seems to be the result of uneven watering and follows on from periods of drought interspersed with rain.

Although Cox's Orange Pippin is one of the most popular of all apple varieties it is not a good choice for the colder parts of the country

Apricots

The apricot is usually thought of as a poor relation of the peach, but for those who like its coarser texture and rather different flavour, the fresh fruits are ample reward for the little trouble it takes to grow the tree.

Selected varieties

By far the most widely grown variety is an old one called Moorpark which bears fruits for picking in August and September. New Large Early will mature in early to mid-July and Royal and Shipley (also known as Blenheim) in August.

Pollination

Most varieties of apricot are self-fertile and will set a satisfactory crop if grown as single trees. They do flower early though – usually in March – and as very few bees are about at that time it is usual to go round the flowers with either a rabbit's tail or a soft camel-hair paintbrush to distribute the pollen. I also think that it is a good idea to give the flowers some protection from frost at this time by hanging some rough hessian or string netting over the branches – taking care, of course, not to knock off the flowers.

Rootstocks

Apricots are usually budded on to plum rootstocks. For smaller trees St Julien A is used and for larger free-standing trees either Brompton or Common Mussel.

Soil and situation

A sunny and sheltered position is necessary for apricots – they do not have the strongest of constitutions. A south- or south-west-facing wall is ideal or a border in a greenhouse if you can spare the room.

Apricots are not at all happy in heavy, waterlogged soils; choose a deep, well-drained light soil for preference but one which will not

Apricots can be grown against a sunny wall. This variety is Moorpark

dry out too rapidly. Plenty of well-rotted manure or garden compost should be added to help in the matter of water retention and to give the trees the nourishment they require.

Forms of tree

Though the apricot can be grown as a bush, I think that it is much more satisfactory to grow it as a fan-trained specimen either in a lean-to greenhouse against the back wall or out of doors against the house. It is possible – though not many are seen nowadays – to grow standard specimens but these do not fruit well. Pot-grown apricots are an easy solution if you have a greenhouse with limited space (see page 81).

Choose a south or south-west-facing wall for fan-trained apricots or grow them in a greenhouse

Planting

As the buds of the apricot break early it is best if the trees are planted in autumn to give them time to settle in before flowering. Plant two- to three-year-old trees which have already had formative training, positioning them so that the base of the main stem is about 30 cm (12 in) from the wall. Plant 5·5 to 7·5 m (18 to 24 ft) apart depending on the rootstock used. If the soil is very acid a dressing of lime should be applied now, and then every spring, to assist stoning. (Stones which do not form properly result in imperfect fruits.)

Supporting wires should be attached to the wall through vine eyes, which will hold the strands some 8 cm (3 in) away from the brickwork. The wires should be arranged horizontally so that one occurs about every 30 cm (12 in) up the wall.

Cover the roots with about 8 cm (3 in) of soil and firm the tree in well. Tie the branch framework to canes, which in turn are tied to the wires, see page 79.

Training and pruning

As with all trained trees the object of pruning is to encourage the production of both fruiting wood and growths to replace old, worn-out branches which form the basic framework of the tree.

Apricots fruit both on two-year-old shoots and on the spurs produced on the older branches. Most of the pruning is done in summer and begins in early summer when buds which are badly placed are rubbed out. These consist of any which are shooting straight out from the wall or in places where they would cause overcrowding. Later in the summer, from mid-July onwards when they have reached pencil thickness, shorten the side shoots to four or five leaves.

In winter, the leading shoots can be shortened as much as is necessary to keep them within bounds and the side shoots are tied in if there is room for them or shortened to three buds.

Fruit thinning. This is not usually necessary, but if the fruits appear to be very close together wait until stoning has taken place and then thin them to leave one every 8 or 10 cm (3 or 4 in). Check that the stones have formed by cutting one of the fruits open. Some of the fruits may drop shortly after setting and if you thin too early you will lose more than you bargained for.

Feeding

With greenhouse-grown trees soak the borders whenever the soil is on the dry side and apply a liquid feed once a month during the growing season. Outdoor trees should be given a dressing of rose fertilizer in February or March. Trees growing both indoors and out of doors will welcome a mulch of well-rotted manure or compost in April.

Soak the soil in which the outdoor crop is growing when the fruits are about the size of small marbles; this will help to prevent the fruits from falling prematurely.

Harvesting

The fruits will colour well some time before they are ripe, but you will feel the flesh begin to soften as ripening progresses. Pick the fruits just before they are fully ripe, removing them with a short stalk, and bring them inside to finish ripening. This prevents them from making a meal for the wasps.

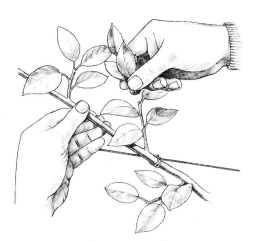

To encourage the formation of fruiting spurs pinch back the laterals in summer to four or five leaves

Storing. Apricots will not store fresh, but they can be used as soon as they are ripe in jams and chutneys. They will freeze if the stones are removed.

Pests and diseases

Aphids and red spider mites are the most common pests and die back and brown rot the two most likely diseases. Silver leaf may be a problem but this is quite rare in apricots.

See pages 120 to 123.

Blackberries

There is no better way of indulging a liking for blackberry and apple pie than by growing one of the cultivated blackberries. These produce larger fruits than the wild brambles and the picking is less hazardous – particularly if you choose a thornless variety. Apart from this they can be put to good use to form barriers between different parts of the garden if trained on horizontal wires; or, in a small garden, one or two can be accommodated against a wall, even a north-facing one is suitable, or on the side of a garage or garden shed.

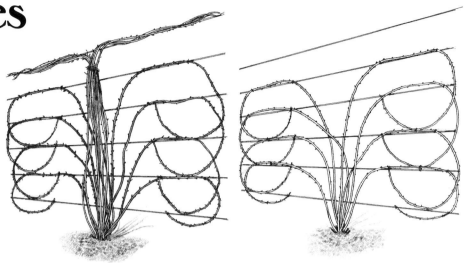

When training blackberry and loganberry canes keep the new and old canes apart by taking the new ones up the centre. When the old canes have been pruned, lower the new ones into position

Selected varieties

There are a number to choose from. Oregon Thornless and Merton Thornless (mid-season) have good quality berries as well as the obvious attraction of no thorns. Himalayan Giant is a very vigorous variety and a heavy cropper but it is particularly vicious with large thorns (early to mid-season). The Parsley-leaved or Cut-leaved blackberry offers ornamental foliage as well as good berries (mid- to late season). Bedford Giant (early season) bears large fruit but not of such good flavour. John Innes is late season and one of the best, with sweet, well-flavoured berries.

Soil and situation

Blackberries are very easy to grow in any soil except, perhaps, a dry, sandy one, and although they do best in a sunny position they will stand shade provided it is not too dry.

However, I find that good soil preparation does pay off in increased crops and I like to dig in plenty of organic matter in the form of well-rotted manure or garden compost before planting as this helps to create a moisture-retentive layer.

Planting

Planting can take place any time during the autumn and winter when the weather is reasonable. Spread the roots well, covering them with at least 5 cm (2 in) of soil and allowing 3 m (10 ft) between plants. In order to build up strong plants it is better not to try to take a crop the first summer and instead to cut the canes down to 23 cm (9 in) at planting time.

Blackberries are rambling plants and need some form of support. They can be trained against hori-

Berries of the variety Himalayan Giant

zontal wires stretched between strong posts or against walls or trelliscs, but when fully grown they are heavy and the supporting material must be both strong and secure.

Training and pruning

The flowers and fruit are carried on the one-year-old canes and the pruning, which is not at all complicated, is aimed at encouraging the production of healthy young canes. It is carried out as soon as the fruit has been picked.

At this stage all the canes which have borne fruit are cut out at ground level and the new young canes are trained in to take their place. There are several ways of training the canes but I find that the following is one of the simplest.

Each year the new canes as they grow are trained up the centre and across the top of the fruiting canes and are lightly tied in position. Then, when the older canes have been cut out, they are untied and brought lower into a fan shape with the ends of each cane looped around. This leaves the centre of the plant free for the new canes which will develop in the next season.

Cultivation

Very little routine cultivation is needed – a dressing of general fertilizer in spring followed by a mulch of well-rotted garden compost or manure being the main requirements.

Propagation

Blackberries are easily increased by tip layering in July. This is done by bending down the tips of some of the strong new growths and anchoring them in the soil with bent wires or stones. The rooted tips and young plants can be severed from the parent and lifted for replanting in the spring.

Harvesting and storing

Pick when the berries are firm and fully coloured. Blackberries, like other cane fruit, freeze well.

Loganberries are a useful soft fruit which ripen after the maincrop raspberries

Pests and diseases

The grubs of the raspberry beetle are likely to be a problem. Control by dusting with derris at petal fall and again two weeks later.

Cane spot, a disease of raspberries, is also seen on blackberries and loganberries. For control see page 120.

Stunting of the canes is a symptom of virus disease and the only control is by lifting and burning diseased plants.

Blackberries and loganberries can be propagated by inserting the tip of a cane into the soil and pegging it in position

Loganberries

Loganberries are hybrid berries which number the blackberry among their parentage. They are a most useful crop for providing continuity of soft fruit production, ripening as they do in late July and August after the maincrop raspberries.

The large well-formed berries have a slightly tart flavour. To make sure that you obtain good cropping plants look out for the two best strains, LY 59 and the thornless L654.

Cultivation

Loganberries are grown and treated in the same way as blackberries.

Harvesting and storing

The berries are dark red when ripe and, once again, they freeze extremely well.

Pests and diseases

Loganberries are affected by the same pests and diseases as blackberries.

91

Cherries

Although cherries are delicious when eaten straight from the tree, I think they are particularly fine when used as pie fillings and to make jams. The acid Morello cherry is excellent for cooking.

Selected varieties

Variety	Colour	Use	Season
Black Heart	Blackish red	D	July
Bigarreau de Schrecken	Reddish black	D	June
Bigarreau Napoleon	Yellow and red	D	August
Early Rivers	Black	D	June
Elton Heart	Yellow and red	D	July
Kent Bigarreau	Yellow and red	D	July
Kentish Red	Red	C	July
Merton Favourite	Black	D	July
Morello	Reddish black	C	August & September

D = dessert or sweet cherry   C = culinary or acid cherry

Pollination

Nearly all the sweet cherries are self-sterile and at least two different varieties should be planted if the trees are to crop at all. The following are successful combinations: Bigarreau de Schrecken and Elton Heart or Early Rivers; Early Rivers and Merton Favourite or Bigarreau de Schrecken; Merton Favourite and Early Rivers or Elton Heart; Bigarreau Napoleon and Kent Bigarreau or Elton Heart.

By far the most widely grown of the acid cherries is Morello, which is self-fertile. Kentish Red is also self-fertile.

Rootstocks

Both sweet and acid cherries are budded or grafted on to Mazzard stocks (sometimes known as the common gean or wild cherry), and the one identified as F12/1 is the best as it is resistant to bacterial canker.

Soil and situation

Flowering as early as they do, cherries are liable to have their flowers damaged by frost in low-lying areas, so it is important to avoid planting them on a site where cold air is collected such as in low valleys and frost pockets formed by buildings and hedges. Cherries will grow well on east- or west-facing walls, and acid cherries even on one which faces north.

For preference, select a well-drained soil which has previously been well cultivated. Deep soils overlying chalk are particularly suitable as the chalk helps the fruits to stone well. A good application of well-rotted manure in the autumn before planting will be very beneficial.

Forms of tree

The sweet cherries are usually grown as standards and such large trees are impossible to accommodate in a small garden, but they can also be grown as fan-trained specimens.

Acid cherries are, to my mind, most successfully and most usefully grown as fan-trained trees, although they can be grown as bushes and small standards.

Planting

The planting of trees lifted from the open ground may be carried out at any time in autumn or winter, although early November is, I think, the best month. Container-grown trees can be put in at any time. Details of planting will be found on page 77.

It is a good idea to buy two- or three-year-old trained trees as they will save you a lot of trouble in the formative years; however, if you do buy a maiden tree then the method of fan training is given on page 107.

Fan-trained trees will need to be spaced 4·5 to 5·5 m (15 to 18 ft) apart; standards 9 m (30 ft) apart and bushes 4·5 m (15 ft) apart.

Training and pruning

The main difference between sweet and acid cherries, apart from the obvious one of taste, is that they fruit on different wood: the sweet on spurs which are generally produced on older wood, and the acid on the previous year's growth – one-year-old wood. For this reason the pruning methods are different, though the training of fan-trained specimens – tying in laterals and removing those which are weak or will cause overcrowding – is basically the same.

Like plums, cherries are susceptible to silver leaf and so it is best to prune them in spring and summer to lessen the likelihood of attack. Paint all large pruning cuts with a bituminous paint.

Pruning sweet cherries. Although established standard or bush sweet cherries should be pruned as little as possible they will generally need some cutting back in the early stages to build up a good branch formation. This involves

The acid Morello cherry will produce a good crop of fruit even when grown on a north-facing wall

cutting back the leaders to about half of their length and either removing weak shoots completely or cutting them back to 5 or 8 cm (2 or 3 in). Once the required number of strong well-spaced branches have been formed then it will only be necessary to cut out crossing and overcrowded growths and any dead wood. If the leaders start to become weak they can be shortened by a third.

Wall-trained trees will need rather more pruning. The main framework is built up in the same way as the peach. Space the branches out evenly and tie in new ones to the supporting wires at about 30-cm (12-in) intervals. When the leading shoots reach the top of the wall either take out each growing point back to a suitable lateral, or bend each shoot downwards until it almost forms a circle, and tie this in to the wires. By doing this you will reduce the vigour of the leading shoots and force some of the laterals to break and become more fruitful.

Early in the summer rub out any shoots which are growing towards the wall or directly outwards from the branches. All the other laterals should either be tied in, if they are to be trained as part of the framework, or shortened to five or six leaves in July if they are to be kept for fruit production.

Immediately after fruiting any dead wood can be removed and the laterals which were shortened in July cut back to three or four buds. Excessively long shoots can be tipped back or tied down in a horizontal position.

Pruning acid cherries. Here the aim is to maintain a constant supply of new wood and, although the initial pruning of bush trees is the same as for sweet cherries, once the trees are established some of the branches must be cut back each year into the old wood. This treatment induces fresh growth from the dormant buds. Pruning of this kind is best done in the spring as soon as growth begins.

The pruning of wall-trained acid cherries is again similar to that of the fan-trained peach. The main branches should be cut back by about a third at planting time to encourage the laterals to break. Each year the older branches should be shortened a little and the resulting young shoots tied in to the framework. Those which are to act as main stems can be allowed to grow longer. Thin out some of the older wood each year after the crop has been picked.

Cultivation

I like to apply a dressing of rose fertilizer (which is high in potash) in February or March. A mulch of manure or garden compost in April will suit them as well, and this also helps to stop the soil from drying out (borders against walls have a habit of drying out quite rapidly) and this, coupled with occasional good waterings will keep the cherries happy.

As the fruits are beginning to form you would be wise to provide some kind of protection from birds – so many crops are ruined by bullfinches and pigeons. Large nets draped over the branches or fruit cages are the best methods of discouraging them. Thinning the fruits will not be necessary.

Harvesting

Pick the fruits as soon as they are ripe – you can test them at intervals – and eat or preserve them as soon as possible.

Storing. Cherries will not store like apples or pears, but they will freeze quite well if the stones are removed.

Pests and diseases

Birds and aphids are the most damaging pests, but slugworm and winter moth may occasionally be a nuisance. Bacterial canker, brown rot, die back, silver leaf and witches broom are the likely diseases.

See pages 120 to 123.

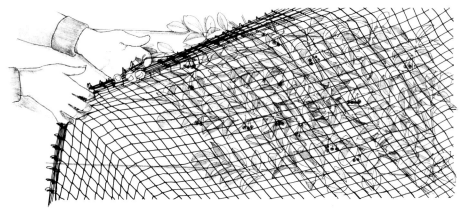

Cherries are a favourite food of the birds and will need the protection of fruit nets

Currants

As a group, the currants provide us with some of the most useful soft fruit. They are ideal for pie making and come into their own when used in preserves and jellies. Although the fruits are similar in all three kinds, the culture of black currants is different from that of the red and white kinds.

Selected varieties

Black currant
Boskoop Giant – early
Mendip Cross – early
Seabrook's Black – mid-season
Wellington XXX – mid-season
Baldwin – late

Red currant
Laxton's No. 1 – early
Red Lake – mid-season

White currant
White Dutch – mid-season
White Versailles – mid-season

Pollination

All the currants, black, red and white, are self-fertile so single bushes can be grown.

Soil and situation

All currants will give of their best on an open and sunny site and it is essential that the ground they occupy is well drained and yet capable of retaining an adequate amount of moisture; thin, dry soils are not to their liking.

Dig the ground they are to occupy in autumn and incorporate as much manure, peat or good garden compost as possible. Even a dry sandy soil can be made suitable if enough organic matter is worked into the top 45 cm (18 in).

Planting

Plant only stock which is known to be in good health. Black currants are sold as two-year-old bushes certified free from virus diseases and these are the ones you should buy

Black currants are the most useful of the three kinds of currants. They are not difficult to grow and deserve a place in the garden

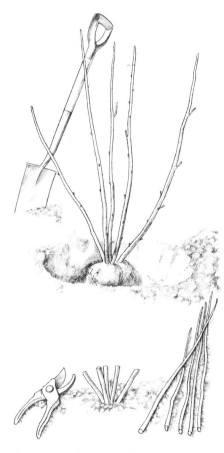

Planting black currants These are grown as bushes with a number of stems coming from the roots. Plant the bushes a few inches deeper than they were growing in the nursery and firm them in well. After planting shorten all the stems

for preference. It is possible to obtain one-year-old bushes but they will not be certified.

No such scheme operates for red and white currants, which are also available as cordon-trained plants, so be sure to obtain these from a reputable supplier.

Planting is carried out in the orthodox season, that is, from November to March, and the bushes will get off to a better start if the land is given a dressing of a general fertilizer mixed with a similar amount of bonemeal and applied at the rate of 110 g per square metre (4 oz per square yard). Firm the bushes well. Allow 1·5 m (5 ft) between the plants in the rows and the same between the rows – planting them square in fact. For the planting and training of cordons, see gooseberries.

Black currants should always be planted a few inches deeper than they were when growing in the nursery so that the bases of the branches are under the soil. If this is done they will form good, strong growth from the base.

Red and white currants should be planted to the same depth as

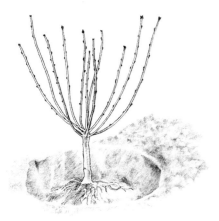

Planting red and white currants Place the bush in position and return and firm in the soil. Immediately after planting the branches should be cut back to an outward-facing bud

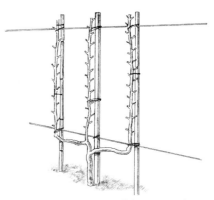

The method of training a triple-stemmed cordon red or white currant

they were growing previously. Those not trained as cordons are grown on a short 'leg' or bare main stem.

Training and pruning

In the first year after planting the plant's energy should be spent in producing stems rather than fruit, so immediately after planting the bushes should be pruned.

With black currants this involves cutting all the stems to within 15 cm (6 in) of the ground to allow a good

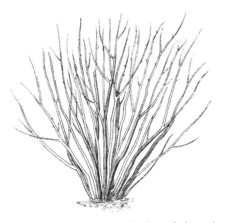

Pruning black currants As these fruit on the one-year-old wood the object of pruning is to remove as much of the older wood each year as possible. *Left* An unpruned bush. *Right* After pruning

Laxton's No. 1 is a popular early cropping variety of red currant

framework of young fruiting wood to grow up in the first year. Black currants produce their best fruit on one-year-old wood.

Subsequent pruning of black currants entails the systematic removal of a portion of the old wood each year after the fruit has been picked. This is best done by cutting out most of the wood which has just carried fruit.

Newly planted red and white currants should be reduced by half: each branch being cut back to half its original length at an outward-facing bud. Unlike the black currant which bears all its fruit on stems which were formed the previous year, red and white currants fruit on spurs which are produced on old wood as well as on the young wood.

Pruning of established red and white currants involves the cutting back of the laterals to within about six leaves of the main branches in July. Only five or six main branches should be retained at any one time

It is important when pruning black currants to distinguish between the old and new wood

and new growths should be allowed to replace them at the rate of one or two each year – always try to keep the centre of the bush open by removing inward growing and crossing branches. This removal of the older branches should be done in winter and at the same time the length of the main young branches should be reduced by half and the laterals shortened back to two or three buds.

Cordons should have the laterals shortened to five or six leaves in summer. In late autumn these summer-pruned laterals are cut back further to two or three buds. The leaders are left unpruned until they have reached the desired height.

Cultivation

Mulching is beneficial to all currants – especially if it is carried out in spring when it has the opportunity of keeping the moisture in the soil as well as adding nutrients. A dressing of sulphate of potash or a rose fertilizer applied at the rate of 25 g per square metre (1 oz per square yard) will give them a boost if applied in April, and black currants also appreciate a dressing of sulphate of ammonia at the same rate; this supplies nitrogen which is essential for the production of new growth. A general feed is also beneficial after fruiting.

Water generously whenever the soil shows signs of drying out and hoe lightly between the rows to keep down weeds. Herbicides can be used if hoeing is impractical.

Propagation

Propagation of currants by hardwood cuttings is quite easy. In October or November, select some sturdy young growths and trim them to a length of 23 to 30 cm (9 to 12 in). Leave all the buds on the black currant cuttings but remove all but the top four or five on the red and white. Take out a 15-cm (6-in) deep trench on a suitable piece of cultivated land and line the bottom with sand. Insert the cuttings to two-thirds of their depth and return the soil, making sure that it is firm. Roots will have formed by the following year and the plants will be ready for setting out in the following autumn.

Harvesting and storing

The fruit should be picked as soon as it is ripe and if it is not going to be eaten immediately take the strig (the small cluster of stalks which holds the berries) as well. If they are to be taken straight to the table the berries can be pulled and the strig left on the plant.

All the currants freeze well.

Pests and diseases

The biggest problem with black currants is the reversion virus carried by the big bud mite. This is so prevalent that it is worth carrying out routine sprays with lime sulphur every year even before the pest or disease is encountered.

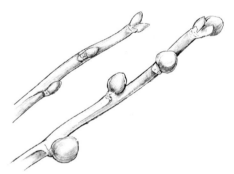
The lower twig shows buds which have been affected by big bud mite. This is a serious problem and routine spraying is important

Spray when the foliage is about 2·5 cm (1 in) in diameter. Other likely pests are aphids, birds and capsid bugs. The most widespread diseases are leaf spot and rust.

Red and white currants fall prey to birds, aphids, leaf spot and coral spot.

See pages 120 to 123.

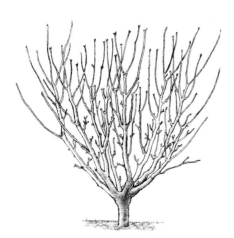
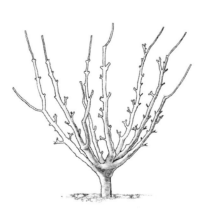
Pruning red and white currants These fruit on spurs and pruning involves reducing the length of the main branches and shortening the laterals. *Left* Unpruned. *Right* Pruned

Figs

Apart from its rich fruits, the fig is well worth growing as an ornamental tree – its fingered leaves have an imposing appearance, especially if the tree is planted alongside more delicate shrubs.

Selected varieties

The best and most widely available variety is Brown Turkey which has dark brown fruits, when ripe, with deep red flesh. White Marseilles is a good substitute if this is not available.

Brown Turkey, one of the best fig varieties

Soil and situation

Figs are not very hardy subjects and for this reason you should provide them with a sheltered site. This does not mean that they should be placed in a shady corner, for as well as protection from winds they need lots of sunshine to ripen the fruits. In very mild areas the trees may be grown as free-standing specimens, but to be on the safe side they are best planted against a south- or south-west-facing wall and grown as a fan.

If given a rich soil and left to its own devices, the fig would quickly form a large tree but it would not produce much in the way of fruit, so for this reason it is customary to restrict its root run.

You can do this by making a hole about 1 m (3 ft) square and lining it with corrugated iron, asbestos or flagstones. Alternatively, and this is perhaps more easily carried out, a large tank or barrel can be sunk into the ground – (don't forget to make some holes in the bottom of the container for drainage) – and filled with good soil. This will give the roots adequate nourishment and yet confine them to a suitable area.

Planting

Plant the tree within the restricted area, spreading out the roots and firming the soil well. Trim off any damaged roots. Planting is best carried out in late November if you have a choice, but any time from

The distinctive leaves of the fig tree give it an added attraction as a decorative plant. The drawing shows two kinds of fig – the larger ones which are nearly ready for harvesting and the smaller ones which will not ripen before the frosts

late October to mid-March is satisfactory. Plants grown in containers can be planted at any time of year but do make sure that you give them adequate supplies of water if they are planted in the summer months. Allow at least 4·5 m (15 ft) between fan-trained trees.

To encourage the production of fruit, the roots must be restricted. Here the planting hole is lined with paving slabs

Training and pruning

Wires attached to the wall with vine eyes or large mesh wire or plastic netting supported in a similar manner are equally effective in keeping the tree in shape. A piece of wall no more than 2 or 3 m (6 to 9 ft) wide and of the same height provides enough space and the tree should be carefully pruned so that it takes up no more space than it can conveniently be allowed.

In the first year after planting, remove all the fruits as they start to form so that the strength of the young plant is conserved. Figs are usually fan trained so space out the healthiest branches on the wire or plastic framework and tie them in. Figs fruit on one- and two-year-old wood and this is the kind you should encourage and preserve. As the tree gets older, remove any thin or weak shoots and cut out one or two of the older branches each year back to buds which will sprout again and produce healthy young wood. Do this in autumn as soon as the leaves have fallen. In this way the old, non-cropping branches are systematically removed and a constant supply of young fruiting wood is maintained. Tie the young growths which will carry the next year's crop into the wires.

The one worry you will not have with the fig is pollination, for the fruits will form regardless of whether the flowers have been pollinated or not. The flowers, by the way, are carried inside the young fig. It will be necessary, however, to thin out the fruit, and this is done by removing the young fruits from the top half of the cropping branches. This will encourage the figs on the lower part of the branches to develop better and so be less susceptible to the hard winter weather – this they need to survive in order to ripen properly in the second year. A similar result can be obtained if the side growths which are not needed to extend the main branches are pinched back to five or six leaves in the summer.

Any shoots which show an excess amount of vigour should be pinched back to keep them in bounds; the best fruits are always produced on shorter, sturdier growths.

Figs grown under glass may carry up to three crops each year, but out of doors one crop is the average with a second being produced in the autumn if it is sunny and warm.

Feeding

A lot of feeding is unnecessary for figs and they will be quite happy if given a mulch of farmyard or stable manure each spring and a few weak liquid feeds throughout the summer whilst the fruits are forming.

Soak the soil in the container whenever necessary; it should never be allowed to dry out.

Harvesting

The figs ripen in late July, August and September and should be picked from the tree as soon as a drip of nectar shows at the tip or as they begin to split. Any fruits which are not fully formed by the beginning of October should be removed for they will never come to anything. The ones which will form next year's crop are on the present year's wood and will be quite small; the ones you will be picking will be on two-year-old wood.

Pests and diseases

Brown scale and mealy bug will be the two most frequently encountered pests and fig canker and botrytis are the most likely diseases.

See pages 120 to 123.

Gooseberries

This useful fruit for both dessert and culinary purposes is easily grown on a wide range of soils. Provided you can save them from the depredations of birds the succulent fully ripe berries of such varieties as Golden Drop, Leveller and Lancer make a fitting end to any meal.

Selected varieties

Variety	Colour	Use	Season
Careless*	Greenish yellow	C	Mid-season
Golden Drop	Yellow	D	Mid-season
Keepsake*	Green	C, D	Early
Lancashire Lad	Red	C, D	Mid-season
Lancer	Yellow-green	C, D	Late
Leveller*	Greenish yellow	C, D	Mid-season
Lord Derby	Red	C, D	Mid-season
Whinham's Industry	Red	C, D	Mid-season
Whitesmith	White	C, D	Early

C = culinary   D = dessert   *recommended for freezing

Pollination

Gooseberries are self-fertile so there is no problem in this direction. However, some varieties flower early and if there are few bees around then it is a good idea to hand pollinate the flowers with a camel-hair brush or a rabbit's tail.

Soil and situation

Although it is worth trying gooseberries on most soils, a moist, well-drained one is the best. Both heavy and light soils will be improved by the addition of some form of bulky organic manure. Dig well and remove any perennial weeds; gooseberries are a surface-rooting crop and only shallow hoeing will be possible later.

Apply a dressing of sulphate of potash immediately before planting.

Planting

This can be done any time during the autumn and winter when conditions are suitable, but I like to get it done in November if possible. Make a hole large enough to accommodate the roots well spread out and cover the roots with at least 8 cm (3 in) of soil. Plant firmly, spacing the bush forms 1·25 to 2 m (4 to 6 ft) apart and the cordons 30, 60 or 90 cm (1, 2 or 3 ft) apart depending on the number of stems.

Gooseberries are usually planted as two- or three-year-old plants and in the form of a bush with a short leg – about 30 cm (12 in) high. However, they can also be grown as single-, double- or triple-stemmed cordons and these will need staking as soon as they are planted. The single-stemmed cordons may be trained on an angle but the double- and triple-stemmed are usually trained vertically. In each instance the leading shoot is shortened when it has reached its allotted height.

Careless, a recommended variety of gooseberry ripening in mid-season

Training and pruning

The first pruning is carried out on newly planted bushes to form a framework of branches. This involves shortening the main shoots by about 8 cm (3 in) and cutting the side shoots back to 5 cm (2 in).

Subsequent winter pruning requires that the young branches are cut back about half way, and in the case of the weeping varieties each branch is cut back to an upward-pointing bud at the top of its arch. The lateral growths are cut back to about 5 cm (2 in) to encourage the formation of fruiting spurs, although some can be left longer if there is room for them to make new branches. All weak shoots and shoots growing into the centre of the bush are removed.

Some gooseberry varieties have a weeping growth habit (left). When pruning these cut each branch to an upward-pointing bud at the top of its arch.

Pruning a gooseberry Cut the young branches back to half and shorten the laterals

When pruning cordons, shorten all laterals to three buds and cut back the leading shoots when these have reached the desired height.

With all forms of gooseberries, I usually carry out a certain amount of pruning in late June, cutting back all the laterals to about five leaves. This helps the formation of fruit buds.

Remove any basal growths which appear from ground level.

Cultivation

Weeds must be kept down but any hoeing must be done with care as gooseberry roots are near the surface. Mulching is important and in early spring I apply a topdressing of well-rotted manure or garden compost. Adequate supplies of potash are also necessary and I find a small application of sulphate of potash (or a rose fertilizer) in spring, followed by another one in June will usually be sufficient. It is not necessary to feed with a high nitrogen fertilizer as this encourages the growth of new wood and gooseberries, like red and white currants, fruit on the older wood.

Some form of protection is vital if you wish to harvest your crop rather than having it harvested for you by the birds. Fruit cages offer the best sort of cover, but string or plastic netting spread over the bushes is effective.

Propagation

Gooseberries can be increased by cuttings taken in October and November. Choose 30-cm (12-in) pieces of the current year's growth and remove the tips. As with red currant cuttings, it is also usual to remove all the lower buds leaving four or five only at the top. Insert the cuttings in a straight-sided

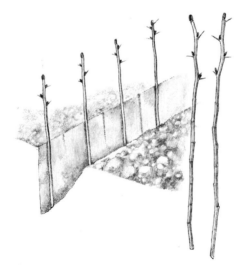

Gooseberry cuttings lined out in a trench. Only four buds are left on each one

trench which has a thin layer of sand in the bottom, spacing them 15 cm (6 in) apart and about 15 cm (6 in) deep. Firm them in well and then leave them for a year before lifting and replanting them.

Harvesting and storing

When good crops are being carried the fruits can be thinned before they are fully mature and the thinnings used for cooking. The remainder can be allowed to grow on until they are fully coloured and 'give' slightly to the touch.

Freezing and bottling are good ways of storing excess berries.

Pests and diseases

As I have already mentioned, birds are likely to be the main pests both of the ripe fruits and, in the case of bullfinches, of the buds. But insects which are capable of wreaking havoc are the caterpillars of the gooseberry sawfly. Keep a close watch for these from May and suspect their presence if you see badly eaten leaves. Spray with derris at the first signs of damage.

American gooseberry mildew is the worst disease, covering leaves, stems and fruits with a felt-like greyish coating; unfortunately it has been especially prevalent in the last few years. The European gooseberry mildew produces a powdery white coating on the leaves. These two diseases can be controlled by spraying with lime sulphur. The varieties Careless, Golden Drop and Leveller are adversely affected by sulphur and mildew on these varieties should be controlled with washing soda and soft soap or dinocap.

See pages 120 to 123.

Grapes

Grapes are, perhaps surprisingly, a versatile crop which can be grown in the greenhouse, sun lounge or conservatory; in pots and containers, and some of the hardier varieties will also grow out of doors. In this book, however, I intend to deal only with growing grapes under glass.

Selected varieties

Black Hamburgh is undoubtedly the best for use in pots and under glass. Buckland Sweetwater is a good white kind; Madresfield Court (black) and Foster's Seedling (white) are among other possibilities, but I would always plump for the first. Muscat of Alexandria is a delicious grape but it is more difficult to grow.

Soil and situation

When growing grapes under glass I am against the idea of planting the root outside the greenhouse where there is little control over it. If the root is planted in a border inside then you have complete control over the watering, feeding and temperature of the soil.

The preparation of the border must be thorough and I would recommend digging it out to a depth of at least 60 to 75 cm (2 to 2½ ft) and placing in the bottom a layer of broken bricks or clinker ash to provide the necessary drainage. On top of this should go a mixture of soil, peat and sand, and for this I use John Innes potting compost No. 3 with an additional dressing of bonemeal.

Planting

The orthodox planting season is between November and March, and with pot-grown specimens it is usual to tease the roots gently apart before placing them in the prepared hole. Cover the roots with about 10 cm (4 in) of soil, firm well and water. Container-grown vines can be planted at any time of the year.

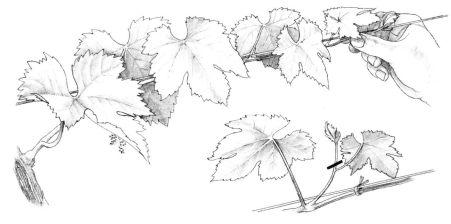

Correct pruning and training is an important part of grape cultivation. The laterals should be pinched out above the fifth or sixth leaf (top), and the sub-laterals should be stopped above the first leaf

The distance between vines depends on the space available and should be 1 m (3 ft) if one rod is to be taken up, 1·5 m (5 ft) if two rods are to be trained.

One plant will be sufficient for the average greenhouse. In the 5·5-m (18-ft) long lean-to greenhouse at the west-facing end of my house I have one plant of Black Hamburgh which, after nine years, is nearly filling the house. The main rod is trained along under the ridge with the fruiting laterals spread out on either side.

Training and pruning

This is the most important part of grape vine culture. In the simplest system the main rod from each plant is trained upwards under the roof to the apex of the house. The laterals are restricted by rubbing out the buds to leave one every 23 cm (9 in), and these are tied into wires strained at 45-cm (18-in) intervals along the length of the house and 23 cm (8 in) away from the glass.

The method of training is as follows. When growth starts in the spring after planting one shoot growing from the top of the vine is allowed to extend upwards and along the length of the greenhouse and is tied, in the initial stage, to a supporting cane. This becomes the main rod and each year until the rod is long enough, one bud at the top is allowed to grow to form the extension.

The laterals are pinched out above the fifth or sixth leaf and the resulting sub-laterals pinched above the first leaf. Although the young vine makes a lot of growth in its first year it will not produce fruit before the second or third year.

In winter, when all the leaves have turned yellow and fallen, the laterals are pruned back to about 2·5 cm (1 in) or two buds from their base and the leading shoot is reduced to a third of its length; for example, if the young rod has made 2 to 3 m (6 to 9 ft) of growth it is reduced to 60 or 90 cm (2 to 3 ft). In this way the length of the rod is extended by 60 or 90 cm (2 or 3 ft) each year.

As I have already said an average greenhouse will take one vine, but if there is more room available other systems of training can be used. Instead of allowing one rod to grow up, two or even three rods can be trained from one vine, each being treated as previously described. There must be a space of 60 to 90 cm (2 to 3 ft) between each rod. Alternatively, the main rod can be trained along the bottom of the house at the height of the eaves and at intervals of approximately 1 m (3 ft) a subsidiary rod is trained up over the top of the greenhouse.

Starting into growth

It is important that the vine remains completely dormant in winter otherwise the sap will start to flow and bleeding will occur, so at this time no heat is given.

If heat is available, some can be put on in late January and this will encourage the young laterals to begin to grow in February or March. The temperature should be about 7°C (45°F) to begin with and this should be increased to 16°C (60°F) after a few weeks.

In an unheated house it will be April to May before growth begins. At this time the leading shoot will be growing and putting out laterals. These are very brittle and easily broken off, so in order to tie them into the wires a piece of raffia is put around each one and this is used to pull the lateral down gradually, only an inch or two each day, until it can be tied to the wire. The tips are pinched out at the fifth or sixth leaf and pruning proceeds as before.

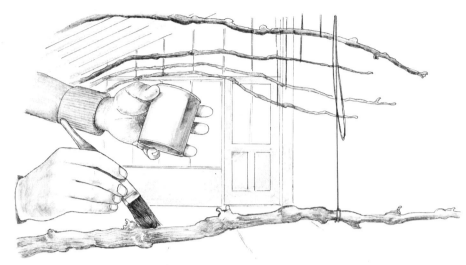

When the vine is completely dormant the rods can be lowered from the greenhouse roof and cleaned. Remove any loose bark and paint the rods with tar oil wash

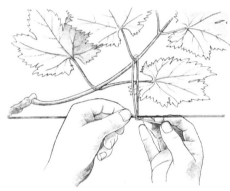

The laterals are very brittle and care is needed when tying them to the wires or they will break. Place a loop of raffia around each one and tighten it daily

One cause of failure is neglecting to give sufficient water. I recommend leaving the hosepipe running for three to four hours over the roots. If you do this once every four weeks or so then the vine will get all the moisture it needs. It is also essential to keep the humidity up by damping down, and later by spraying the vine, always doing this with tepid water.

When flowers are produced a light spraying with water at midday will help the setting of the grapes. Feed when the berries begin to form, sprinkling the fertilizer, and I use one intended for roses, at 110 g to the square metre (4 oz to the square yard) over the root area. Do this once a month until the berries have almost reached maturity.

Fruit thinning

This is done when the grapes are as large as peas and the important thing to remember is not to touch the young berries with the fingers as this spoils the natural bloom. Instead, use a piece of forked stick to lift the berries and a pair of grape scissors to do the cutting. First, cut out all the berries forming inside the bunch and all the small berries which will be seedless. Continue thinning in this way to leave 1 cm ($\frac{1}{2}$ in) between each berry, this allows room for swelling and stops the grapes splitting. You may have to thin out the bunches too, I find that 30 is about the right number for my vine to carry. A good average is to allow 450 to 675 g (1 to $1\frac{1}{2}$ lb) of fruit to each 30 cm (1 ft) of rod.

Thinning a bunch of grapes

Ripening

In August and early September ventilate the house less freely so that the increase in heat will help to ripen the grapes. Do no damping down at this time.

The bunches can be kept for several weeks in a dry room if they are cut with a short length of stem and one end of this is inserted in a bottle filled with water.

Resting the vines

The vines need a period of about three months rest after the grapes have been harvested. Keep the border fairly dry and ventilate freely to keep the temperature down so that the vine remains dormant.

Take this opportunity to clean the rod thoroughly, removing all loose bark which may be harbouring mealy bug or the eggs of aphids and red spider mite. Paint the dormant rod with tar oil winter wash.

Propagation

Vines can be propagated from the growths removed during pruning. The strongest of these are bundled together and put out of doors in a place where they can be partly buried in the soil.

In February they are lifted and cut up into pieces of stem each carrying a single bud or 'eye'. These vine eyes, as they are called, are half buried in sandy soil in 8-cm (3-in) pots, which are then kept in a propagating frame in a temperature of 18°C (65°F) until growth begins. It takes about six weeks for a good root system to form.

Black Hamburgh is the best grape variety for growing under glass

The young plants can be planted in the border in summer or transferred to 13- or 15-cm (5- or 6-in) pots. In the following winter they can either be transplanted to the border or grown on as pot plants.

Propagating grapes Cut the prunings into pieces of stem each carrying one bud or eye (left), and place each bud on a pot of sandy compost

Pests and diseases

The main pests are red spider mite, mealy bug and aphid, and the most important disease is mildew. See pages 120 to 123.

Other troubles. Certain physiological disorders can be a problem.

Shanking is recognized by the fruit stalks shrivelling and dying before the berries ripen. As a result the berries wither. It can be caused by a number of factors: overcropping, or the soil becoming waterlogged or impoverished. To help the situation, remake the borders, paying particular attention to the drainage.

Scalding is, at first sight, similar to shanking as in both the berries turn brown and wither. However, in scalding the trouble does not begin with the stalks, which are unaffected. It is usually caused by too high a temperature in the greenhouse and the damage is found on the side of the bunch which gets the most sun. Scorching of the foliage is also brought on by too high a temperature.

Melons

The flavour of home-grown melons so far surpasses that of shop-bought ones that I often wonder why they are not more widely grown. They are not difficult but the real secret is to grow them in a greenhouse or frame.

Selected varieties

I always grow the cantaloupe type because I love the flavour and Dutch Net is a fine variety. Other cantaloupes are Charantais, Ogen and Sweetheart. This last is a newer variety and easier to grow as it is more tolerant of lower temperatures, in fact, it can be grown successfully under cloches. Hero of Lockinge and Superlative are also good.

Seed sowing

Melon seeds can be sown in peat pots or small clay or plastic pots any time from January to the end of May, but I find that April is the most suitable month. A temperature of 18 to 21°C (65 to 70°F) is needed for germination and from an April sowing the seedlings will be ready for transplanting into beds in the greenhouse by the middle to the end of May or into frames in early June.

Planting

I prefer when planting to make up mounds on the greenhouse staging of John Innes potting compost No. 3, allowing one bucketful of compost to each mound and spacing them about 60 cm (2 ft) apart. What I sometimes do if I've got any decayed farmyard manure is to put this on the staging first and then the soil on top; the plants then have a moist layer of manure to root down into.

The important thing when setting out the seedlings is to plant them high, so that the seed leaves are well above the compost, otherwise they are likely to be affected by stem rot.

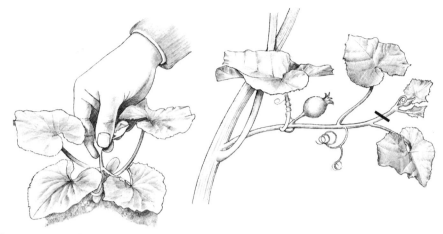

Frame-grown melons should be stopped at the fourth leaf (left). Greenhouse-grown melons are stopped two leaves beyond the fruit (right)

Melons can also be grown in peat bags or large pots, but when grown in pots they will need more watering and feeding.

Training

Each plant is trained straight upwards, supported by a cane if necessary, and the top is pinched out when it reaches the apex of the greenhouse. Horizontal wires, 30 cm (12 in) apart, are stretched down the length of the house approximately 15 cm (6 in) away from the glass, and side shoots are trained out along these. The tip of each side shoot should be pinched out above the second leaf. If a melon forms it will be at the first leaf joint but in the case of the cantaloupes the melons often form on the sub-laterals which grow as a result of the first pinching.

When growing melons in frames the plants are trained horizontally over the ground.

Cultivation

To grow successfully, melons need a minimum temperature of 16°C (60°F) and plenty of water. Watering must, however, be done with care and any water splashes kept away from the base of the plant stems. Keep the atmosphere moist by damping down and spraying over the plants with water.

The melon produces both male and female flowers and it will be necessary to hand pollinate the female ones to get them to set. To do this, remove the male flower (which is distinguished from the female by its slender stalk), then pull off the outside petals to expose the pollen-bearing anthers and place it lightly inside the female flower. This should be done at midday when the pollen is dry.

No more than four fruits should be taken from one plant and it is important for their subsequent growth that all four should be always at the same stage of development. To achieve this the flowers must be pollinated on the same day if at all possible. This can be done by picking off the female flowers until you can select four on different laterals which will open approximately at the same time. You will soon know if the pollination has been successful as the fruits will start to swell within

Pollinating the female flower. This is an essential part of melon culture

a few days. If instead they turn yellow then wait for a new set of female flowers and start again.

Feed weekly with a liquid fertilizer once the fruits start to form, and as soon as white roots show on the surface of the mound topdress with fresh John Innes compost.

Melons are heavy fruit and it will be necessary to support them in string or raffia bags slung from the wires.

Growing in frames

Make a mound of manure and John Innes potting compost No. 3 in the frame exactly as in the greenhouse and plant in this, allowing two plants to each 2 by 1·25 m (6 by 4 ft) frame.

Stop each plant at the fourth rough leaf and train four of the resulting side shoots to the corners of the frame. Remove the tips from the side shoots when they have reached the limits of the frame.

From then on the method of growing is the same as for plants in the greenhouse except that two or three fruits will be sufficient for each plant to carry. Support the melons on pieces of glass or slate to keep them off the soil.

Harvesting and storing

As soon as the melons start to ripen you will be able to smell the aroma and at this stage you should reduce the water supply drastically or the fruits will split.

Melons are heavy fruits and will need to be supported in string bags slung from the wires

Ideally, melons should be eaten when they are fully ripe and at the peak of perfection. However, the flesh will freeze successfully if cut into cubes or balls.

Pests and diseases

Red spider mite is the chief enemy, but keep an eye open for aphids, slugs, snails and mice.

Stem rot is the most serious disease and this can be controlled by careful watering.

These pests and diseases are dealt with under the vegetable section, see pages 70 to 73.

Peaches and Nectarines

Delicious home-grown peaches and nectarines can be raised either out of doors or in a cold greenhouse. Although the nectarine is usually thought of as a different fruit, it is really just a smooth-skinned variety of the peach and has a comparable flavour.

Selected varieties

I have found the following to be good cropping kinds which produce fruits of an excellent flavour.

Peach
Duke of York – July
Hale's Early – July
Peregrine – August
Rochester – August
Dymond – September

Nectarine
Early Rivers – July
Humboldt – August
Lord Napier – August
Pine Apple – September

Pollination

Most varieties of peaches and nectarines are self-fertile and can be grown as individual specimens. Hale's Early, however, needs another variety flowering at the same time for cross pollination purposes.

We cannot always rely on insects for pollination and I think that it is a good idea to give a helping hand when the flowers are open by lightly brushing over them either with a soft paintbrush or with a rabbit's tail, just to make sure that the pollen is distributed. Although not strictly necessary with outdoor crops, this is essential for those grown in the still atmosphere of a greenhouse where pollinating insects are not so abundant. Pollinate at midday and then close the ventilators and damp the floor with water to provide the best conditions for the fertilization of the flowers.

To make sure that the pollen is distributed, brush lightly over the open blossom

Rootstocks

People do, I know, raise peach trees from stones and very successfully too in some cases. If this is done you may get a healthy tree which bears large fruits, but you also stand a fair chance of raising a tree of little vigour which bears small fruits, often of inferior flavour. If you want to be sure of getting good peaches or nectarines and a sturdy tree it is always better to buy from a nurseryman who will have grown the required variety on a suitable rootstock which will give the plant adequate, but not excessive, vigour. The most satisfactory rootstocks are the plum stocks Brompton and St Julien A.

Soil and situation

It is quite possible to grow peaches as bush specimens out of doors, if they are given a warm, sheltered spot, but on the whole it is much safer to grow them against a south-facing wall or fence. Gardens in the north of the country may be too exposed even for wall-trained trees and here the protection of a cold greenhouse is necessary if the fruits are to be saved from the frost.

A heavily manured soil is not needed, but peaches and nectarines will not tolerate badly drained soils, and, if the fruits are to stone well, then very acid soils will need to be given a dressing of lime.

The planting site – whether indoors or out – should be dug to two spades' depth, about 50 cm (20 in), and the bottom of the hole lined with brick rubble to assist drainage if the soil is on the heavy side. Fork in some well-rotted farmyard manure or garden compost. Check the acidity of the soil before adding any lime and do not overdo applications.

Forms of tree

Peaches and nectarines grow best both out of doors and in the cold greenhouse as fan-trained trees. Small bushes can be grown in pots (page 81), and bushes are often successful out of doors in mild areas.

Planting

The general planting instructions are the same as for other top fruit crops, see page 77. Greenhouse-grown trees are best planted against the walls of a lean-to type greenhouse.

Plant any time from November to January – the earlier the better. Space fan-trained trees 5·5 to 7·5 m (18 to 24 ft) apart and bushes 4·5 m (15 ft) apart.

Training and pruning

Peaches and nectarines fruit on one-year-old wood and so the aim in pruning is to have as much new wood as possible formed each year.

When grown as bushes, however, pruning should be reduced to a minimum once the basic framework is established. Maiden trees are pruned as follows. In the May following planting shorten the main stem to about 60 cm (2 ft); select three or four well-placed laterals and cut them back to half – these will form the first main branches; any weak laterals should be cut out.

The next winter the main branches are cut back to half their length; this will result in a lot of new growth and from this about 12 of the best shoots are selected to be treated as leaders – these should cut back to leave 30 cm (12 in) of new wood in the following winter. All other shoots should be cut out. This will give the basic framework of the tree and subsequent pruning involves cutting back any dead wood to a good lateral and removing any crossing branches. If sufficient new wood is not produced then some of the laterals and older branches should be cut back to encourage the dormant buds to break.

As with cherries this pruning is done either in spring when growth starts or immediately the crop has been picked.

Fan-training a young tree. The main stem is cut back to 60 cm (2 ft) in the spring following planting. When growth starts two opposite shoots are selected and allowed to grow whilst all other laterals are

Peregrine, one of the best peach varieties

pinched back. The method of training is shown in the accompanying illustrations.

The shoots are tied to canes, which are in turn secured to the wires, and all other growth is

pinched out. By the early spring of the third year the main framework will consist of eight branches. Each of these is cut back to leave about 75 cm (2½ ft) of new growth, and the previous year's treatment is

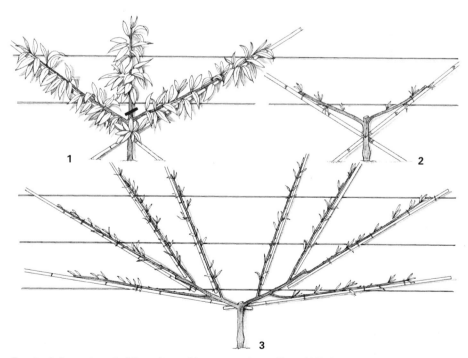

Fan training a tree 1. When the maiden tree starts growing select two strong side shoots about 30 cm (12 in) from the ground and allow these to develop. Pinch back all other shoots and cut out the central stem.

As the side shoots grow tie them to canes at an angle of about 45 degrees. **2.** In the following winter shorten each branch to

about 45 cm (18 in) and, subsequently, allow four shoots to develop on each one in the following positions: one at the tip, two on the upper side and one on the lower side. **3.** As these shoots grow they are tied to canes, and at the end of the third winter the tree should look like this with four branches on each side of the fan

Pruning the mature fan-trained tree involves the use of a system of disbudding to reduce the amount of growth. Pinch off the growth buds on each lateral to leave one at the base, one in the middle and one at the tip

repeated if there is enough wall space.

In the third summer side shoots are allowed to grow at approximately 15-cm (6-in) intervals along the tops of the main branches, any in excess of this and those growing downwards, towards or away from the wall should be rubbed out. These new shoots, which will carry the fruit in the following year, should be tied into the wires and pinched back at 45 cm (18 in). The end bud from each branch should be allowed to continue growing and the resultant new wood tied in.

From then on the pruning follows the replacement system when all shoots which have carried fruits are cut out and the new growths are tied in to become the fruiting wood in the following year. However, in the normal course of events, too much new growth is produced and this must be thinned out by a process of disbudding. This is done over a period of three weeks or so in spring when the trees start into growth. First remove any shoots growing towards or out from the wall and then disbud the young growths of the previous year as shown in the illustration.

After the fruit has been picked cut out any shoots which have just carried fruit unless they are needed for replacement, and remove any dead or diseased wood.

Any suckers which are sent up by the trees should be pulled or cut off close to the roots as soon as they appear.

Fruit thinning

After the fruits have stoned (check this by removing a sample fruit and cutting it open with a knife to see if the stone is forming in the centre) thin them out leaving one every 23 cm (9 in) along the branches. Quite a number of fruits are shed during the stoning period and if they are thinned out before this the crop may be further reduced by such losses.

After the fruits have formed their stones they should be thinned out. In this example the fruits indicated should be removed

Cultivation

Each spring, the tree should be given a dressing of a general fertilizer at the rate of 110 g per square metre (4 oz per square yard) and a light mulch of rotted manure or garden compost. Greenhouse-grown trees will start into growth earlier than those outside and a careful watch should be kept on the thermometer; ventilate whenever the temperature rises above 16°C (60°F). The maximum night temperature should be in the region of 10°C (50°F). Once a month, trees grown in a greenhouse should have their roots flooded with water.

Outdoor trees should be given some protection from frost at flowering time. February is a cold month and the flowering branches should be hung with pieces of string netting and hessian. These can be removed as soon as the fruits have set and the weather begins to be a little milder.

Harvesting

The flesh of peaches and nectarines is very tender and should be handled with great care. Test it by pressing very lightly on the area near the stalk; if this is soft the fruit will probably part quite readily from the tree and this shows that it is ready for eating. If you have to pull the fruit at all it is not ripe.

Storing. The fruits will not keep for any length of time, but they will last a few days if stored in a cool place. Boxes lined with tissues or cotton wool will prevent the skins from being damaged. Peaches and nectarines will freeze if the stones are removed.

Pests and diseases

The pests you will have problems with are aphids, birds and red spider mites – the last named on crops under glass. Of the diseases by far the most widespread is peach leaf curl, although this rarely affects trees grown in a greenhouse. Spray the trees just before the buds break – usually in February – with Bordeaux mixture or a copper fungicide. Do this every year, even if you have not been troubled by the disease; prevention is always better than cure. Silver leaf and die back can occasionally attack.

See pages 120 to 123.

A shoot affected by peach leaf curl

Pears

This is another popular fruit with similar requirements to apples. Pears, however, need a more sheltered site as they flower earlier and so are more likely to be affected by frost. In fact, that best-of-all varieties Doyenné du Comice really needs to be grown in the lee of a south- or south-west facing wall.

Selected varieties

From the wide range of dessert pears available my own choice is as follows. Jargonelle and Williams' Bon Chrétien (early); Louise Bonne of Jersey, Beurré Hardy, Beurré Superfin, Doyenné du Comice, Conference (all mid-season); Joséphine de Malines (an excellent late pear with good flavour). Catillac is a useful variety for cooking, late in season and a good keeper.

Pollination

As with apples it is necessary to take account of the need for cross pollination. In fact, it is even more important as most pear varieties are self-sterile. Conference may sometimes set a crop of rather thin pears without cross pollination but this is also better for having a pollinator.

The table shows a range of varieties together with suggested pollinators.

Pear varieties divided into groups according to the season of flowering. Varieties within the same group will pollinate each other.

Early	Beurré d'Amanlis (T), Emile d'Heyst, Jargonelle (T), Louise Bonne of Jersey
Mid-season	Beurré Superfin, Conference, Durondeau, Joséphine de Malines, Williams' Bon Chrétien
Late	Beurré Hardy, Catillac, Doyenné du Comice, Pitmaston Duchess (T)

T = triploid varieties, not good pollinators

Rootstocks

I have explained earlier (page 76) the need for grafting varieties of top fruit onto a range of rootstocks to control their vigour and time of cropping. In the case of pears the rootstocks used are quince as these not only bring the trees into bearing fairly quickly but also are semi-dwarfing to moderately vigorous in effect and so are suitable for the range of trees which are best for the modern garden, namely bush, dwarf pyramids, cordons, and espaliers.

Malling Quince A is the more vigorous stock while Malling Quince C is moderately dwarfing in effect and brings the trees into cropping slightly earlier, but it is not suitable for espalier trained or bush trees in poor growing conditions.

A difficulty arises, however, in that certain pear varieties will not unite with quince and are what is known as incompatible. In such cases it is necessary to double work the incompatible variety – grafting it onto an intermediate stock taken from a pear variety which will form a union with quince.

Trees on seedling pear stock are available but these make much larger trees which are not suitable for gardens.

Soil and situation

Pears are less tolerant than apples of light sandy soils, preferring as they do the well-drained, moisture-retentive ones. Choose a sunny, sheltered position and prepare the soil by digging it well and adding a dressing of well-rotted manure or garden compost. The ground should have time to settle before planting and immediately before this is done, a dressing of general fertilizer at 110 to 170 g per square metre (4 to 6 oz per square yard) should be scattered over the soil.

Forms of tree

Pears can be grown as bushes, fans, dwarf pyramids, cordons, espaliers.

Williams' Bon Chrétien

With the exception of fans (page 107) all are described on page 83.

Planting

Pears are planted as other trees, see page 77. Spacings for the various forms of tree are as follows:

Bush trees – on Quince A 3·5 to 4·5 m (12 to 15 ft); on Quince C 3 m (10 ft).

Cordons – on either rootstock 1 m (3 ft) apart with 2 m (6 ft) between rows.

Dwarf pyramids – on either rootstock 1 m (3 ft) with 2·25 m (7 ft) between rows.

Espaliers and fans – on Quince A 4·5 m (15 ft); on Quince C 3·5 m (12 ft).

Training and pruning

The pruning of pears is very similar to that of apples but they can be cut back harder without encouraging more vigorous growth. However, it is better to prune young bush trees more lightly than

The ornamental value of a pear tree in full blossom should not be ignored

apples and if necessary to prune more severely only when they have started cropping.

General pruning for the established bush is to cut the laterals back to three or four buds and reduce the fruit buds on the spurs to three or four in number. At the same time the leaders may be shortened by half their length.

The majority of pears form their fruit buds on spurs, but two popular varieties, Jargonelle and

Pears grow well trained as fans or on espaliers and can be used to clothe a large wall

Joséphine de Malines are tip bearers and require care with pruning so that you do not cut back too many of the fruit-bearing laterals.

See page 84 for pruning and training instructions. One difference to note – because pears flower earlier than apples summer pruning of trained trees is carried out rather earlier, starting from early July in the south of the country.

Fruit thinning. The principle of fruit thinning is explained on page 85. On the whole pears need less thinning than apples, any that is required being carried out when the fruitlets begin to turn downwards. To get the best sized fruit

Although pears do not require as much thinning as apples, it is a good idea to remove some of the fruitlets

they should be thinned to leave one or two at the most.

Feeding

Pears will need feeding every spring and for this I like to use a rose fertilizer, applying it at the rate of 110 to 225 g per square metre (4 to 8 oz per square yard) depending on the growth of the tree. An annual light mulch of decayed manure or garden compost will also help to keep the trees in good condition and will cater for their nitrogen requirement which is higher than that of apples.

Harvesting

The best test of whether the pears are ripe enough for picking is to lift a fruit and twist it gently. If it parts readily from the branch then it is ready for picking although not necessarily ripe for eating. With the early and mid-season varieties it is better to pick a little early while the fruit is still green.

Late varieties, although still picked green, should not be picked too early or they will lack flavour and may shrivel.

Storing. Use early pears as soon as possible after picking as they do not store well. Late pears may be stored in a cool dry airy place, but they need to be kept a bit warmer than apples. Do not wrap the fruit

but place it in trays or on slatted shelves. Check the fruit over every few days and use them as soon as they are ripe; this is often indicated by the softening of the flesh near the stem, but it is very difficult to tell for sure when pears are ripe and the only certain way is to cut and try a sample fruit. Once they are ripe they will rapidly go rotten, so frequent checking, once a day, should not be neglected.

Another method of storing pears is by freezing, although this may be accompanied by some loss of texture.

Check stored pears frequently and remove any which show signs of rot

Pests and diseases

Aphids, pear midge, fruit tree red spider, and birds are the main pests. The ripening fruit may be badly infested by wasps and the only way of combating this hazard completely is by protecting the individual fruit in muslin bags.

Canker, mildew, scab and brown rot are the most likely diseases.

The spraying programme for apples given on page 87 can be equally well applied to pears.

See pages 120 to 123.

A fruit affected by pear scab

Plums

Plums and damsons are not as widely grown as apples and pears but they are equally useful. Dessert varieties are delicious eaten fresh from the tree, and the culinary kinds are excellent for preserves and pie making.

Selected varieties

The table shows some well-tried varieties of plums, gages and damsons which are all of value for their different characteristics.

Variety	Size and Colour	Use	Season
Coe's Golden Drop	Medium sized; yellow	D	September
Czar	Medium sized; purplish red	C	Early August
Denniston's Superb	Medium sized; greenish yellow with darker green streaks	D	Mid-August
Early Transparent Gage	Medium to small; yellow with red spots	D	Mid-August
Marjorie's Seedling	Large; purplish black with reddish stalks and white bloom	C to D*	October
Merryweather Damson	Small; black with white bloom	C	September to October
Monarch	Large; dark purple	C	Early September
Oullin's Golden Gage	Large; greenish yellow	C & D	Mid-August
Pershore	Medium sized; yellow	C	Late August
Rivers' Early Prolific	Small; black	C & D	July to August
Shropshire Damson	Medium sized; blue-black	C	September to October
Victoria	Large; plum red	C & D	Mid- to late August

C = culinary   D = dessert   *when fully ripe

Pollination

With the exception of Coe's Golden Drop and Rivers' Early Prolific all the varieties listed here are self-fertile, which means that they can set fruit with their own pollen. Having said that, it is always a good idea to grow more than one tree, if you can, to ensure that pollination is fully effected.

Care must be taken, though, to ensure that the varieties chosen to pollinate each other are both compatible (they can be pollinated with each other's pollen) and in flower at the same time. Coe's Golden Drop, which is an excellent tree for a south-facing wall, must have a pollinator and Rivers' Early Prolific, Denniston's Superb, Monarch, Czar, Merryweather Damson, Pershore and Victoria are all suitable, and all of these will pollinate each other. Rivers' Early Prolific, which is only partially self-fertile, can be pollinated with any of the varieties just mentioned except Monarch which flowers too early.

Marjorie's Seedling and Shropshire Damson will pollinate each other and also Early Transparent Gage and Oullin's Golden Gage. The last two varieties are also in flower at the same time as Czar, Merryweather Damson, Pershore and Victoria.

Rootstocks

Most of the trees sold by nurseries are grafted onto one of the following rootstocks: Brompton, Myrobalan B, Pershore, and St Julien A. The first two are vigorous and are used to produce large trees. St Julien A and Pershore are semi-dwarfing and are the most suitable rootstocks for the small garden and for use where the trees are to be trained as fans.

Soil and situation

The plum is a demanding crop and it will seldom do well if grown on shallow, impoverished ground. Deep, rich soil which will hold an adequate supply of moisture and yet allow excess water to drain away freely is the ideal. Very acid soils are not suitable for plums and in such cases a dressing of lime should be given.

Plums need more nitrogen than apples, especially in the formative years, and appreciate light annual mulches of well-rotted manure. For this reason also, it is better to keep the ground around plum trees cultivated, although you should remember that plums are shallow rooting and weeds should be kept under control with herbicides rather than by hoeing. If you do want to grass down the area then you will need to give extra feeding to make up for the nitrogen taken up from the soil by the grass.

Forms of tree

Bushes and half-standard trees are the kinds most frequently grown in the open, as standards form trees which are too tall to be adequately pruned, sprayed and picked. Fan-trained trees are also available and these can be grown most satisfactorily against a south- or south-west-facing wall (though they will also tolerate northerly or easterly aspects), and in gardens where available space is restricted.

Plums and damsons are occasionally supplied as cordons, but as they are vigorous trees and there is no dwarfing rootstock I do not think that they are really suited to such restricted training.

Planting

The planting of plums is the same as that of other tree fruit, see page 77. Plums may be planted as maidens or partially trained trees of two or three years old.

Half-standard and bush trees on Brompton or Myrobalan B rootstocks should be planted 5·5 to 6 m (18 to 20 ft) apart, and 3·5 to 4·5 m (12 to 15 ft) on St Julien A or Pershore.

Fan-trained trees on St Julien A or Pershore should be 4·5 to 5·5 m (15 to 18 ft) apart.

Training and pruning

Plums require only a minimum of pruning and this should be carried out either in the spring or immediately after fruiting in the late summer or early autumn, rather than in the winter when there is a greater risk of infection by the silver leaf disease.

Young bush and half-standard trees are pruned as for apples (see page 84) in the early stages, but once the trees are well formed it is only necessary to remove weak, diseased or overcrowded branches. Plums fruit on both old and new wood and a balance should be kept between the two kinds.

Plums of the variety Marjorie's Seedling

The framework of the fan-trained plum is built up in the same way as that of the peach (see page 107). Each year some of the laterals are allowed to grow on to extend the main branches and to replace the old non-fruiting wood, which should be cut out. Laterals not

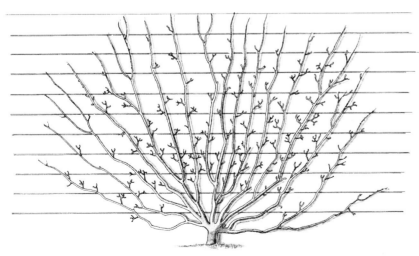

Fan-trained plum trees usually grow best against a warm, sunny wall

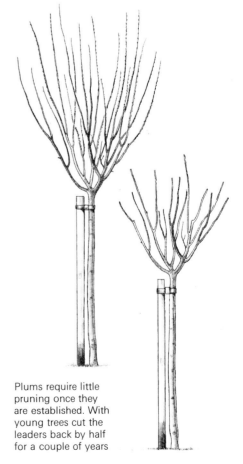

Plums require little pruning once they are established. With young trees cut the leaders back by half for a couple of years

113

Victoria, probably the best known variety of plum

required for extension or replacement should be shortened to about five or six leaves in July. These summer-pruned laterals can be pinched back by about half after the crop has been picked.

Paint all large cuts with a bituminous wound dressing.

Fruit thinning. If the trees crop heavily the fruits should be thinned after the stoning period to leave one every 5 to 8 cm (2 to 3 in) along the branch. Remove one of the fruits and slit it open with a knife to check that the stone has hardened. If fruits are not thinned the crop will be heavier but the tree may not bear the following year.

Cultivation

Heavily laden branches will need propping to prevent them from breaking under the weight of a good crop. This is particularly necessary for such varieties as

Pershore, Rivers' Early Prolific and Victoria which tend to have brittle wood.

If the trees are overfed they will make too much growth and carry less fruit, so give only a light application of fertilizer in February or March. I find that a rose fertilizer is particularly suitable for this purpose. On light soils a mulch of well-rotted manure or garden compost should be applied in April.

Remove any suckers which may grow from the rootstock – pulling them off rather than cutting them if possible.

Harvesting

Damsons and culinary plums can be picked just before they are ripe. You will probably find it best to pick them all at once so that you can go ahead with your jam making or bottling. Dessert plums should be picked when they are fully ripe and the tree should be gone over several times, the ripest plums being removed each time.

Storing. For the best flavour, plums are eaten as soon as they are picked, but there is a way in which you can store them to make the crop last over several weeks. Pick the fruits just before they are ripe and wrap them in greaseproof or waxed paper. Store them in a cool, airy place and take them out for eating as you require them. Check the stored fruits every few days to see if any are ripening and eat these first.

Plums and damsons can be frozen if the stones are first removed. Damsons freeze best as a purée.

Pests and diseases

The most likely pests are aphids, birds, plum sawfly, shot-hole borer, winter moth, and occasionally pear leaf blister mite.

The most devasting disease is silver leaf to which some varieties succumb more than others – Victoria is particularly susceptible. Plums are also liable to attack by bacterial canker, blossom wilt, brown rot, die back and rust.

See pages 120 to 123.

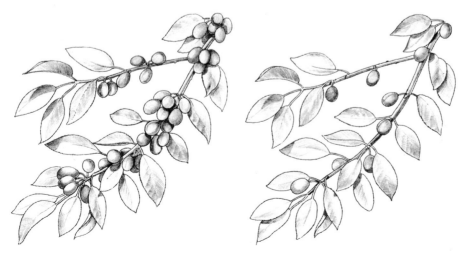

If a plum tree is carrying a heavy crop it is essential to thin the fruit or the plums will be small and lacking in flavour. *Left* Before thinning. *Right* After thinning

Raspberries

This is my favourite soft fruit and surely one of the most useful we grow. Cultivation is relatively easy and certain varieties are ideal for freezing, whilst most of them will make good jams and preserves.

Selected varieties

Glen Clova – early to late
Malling Delight – early to mid-season
Malling Enterprise – mid-season
Malling Exploit – early to mid-season
Malling Jewel – mid-season
Malling Promise – early to mid-season
Norfolk Giant – late
September – autumn
Zeva – autumn

Of these varieties Glen Clova, Malling Exploit and Malling Jewel are especially recommended for freezing and Norfolk Giant and Malling Enterprise for jam making.

Pollination

All raspberries will fruit on their own but will generally bear much better crops if several varieties are grown together. The exception to this rule is Glen Clova which, due to its susceptibility to certain virus infections, should be grown on its own.

Soil and situation

A site sheltered from strong winds is preferred by raspberries but, unlike some fruit crops, they will tolerate a little shade. A slightly acid soil, deeply worked, moist and with adequate supplies of manure, peat or garden compost is ideal.

Planting

Make sure that you obtain healthy plants which are certified free of virus diseases. If present, these diseases will seriously reduce the yield of the crop and spoil your chance of getting a good supply of fruits from the outset.

Before planting, sprinkle a mixture of bonemeal and general fertilizer on the soil in the row at the rate of 110 g per square metre (4 oz per square yard). The canes are going to be producing a lot of growth and fruit and will appreciate the extra feeding.

Space the plants 45 cm (18 in) apart in the row and allow 1·5 m (5 ft) between the rows. Supports must be erected for raspberries and these are best constructed from posts and wire. Insert a stout post at each end of a row (more frequently if the rows are very long) and stretch three horizontal wires between them. The topmost wire will need to be about 1·5 m (5 ft) from the ground (2 m, 6 ft, if Norfolk Giant is being grown) and the other two wires should be spaced evenly below the top one. The canes can be planted any time from November to March and are cut down to within 23 cm (9 in) of the ground in February or March. Be sure to plant them firmly, heeling the soil in well, and cover the roots with about 8 cm (3 in) of soil.

The purpose of the first season's growth is to establish good, sturdy canes for fruiting in the following year, so any flowers which are produced should be picked off. This is only likely to occur with the autumn-fruiting varieties.

Training and pruning

Thin the canes out as they grow and tie them in to the wires. Allow one cane every 15 cm (6 in) or so. If the canes grow beyond the top wire, cut them back to within 8 cm (3 in) of this or bend the tops over and tie them to the wire.

As soon as the fruits of the summer-fruiting varieties are picked – any time between late June and early August – cut out the canes that have fruited at ground level. This should be done as soon as possible so that the young canes which are produced from the roots have time to thicken up and mature before the winter sets in.

Autumn-fruiting raspberries are

When planting raspberries make the hole large enough to hold the roots well spread out and cover the topmost roots with about 5 cm (2 in) of soil

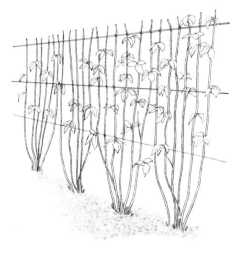

Newly planted raspberry canes should be cut back to 23 cm (9 in) in late winter

When pruning established raspberries cut out the canes which have just fruited

As the new canes grow tie them into the training wires at intervals of 15 cm (6 in)

pruned in the same way in March so that the young canes can grow and ripen through the summer months to produce their crop later in the year.

Cultivation

Keep down the weeds in the row either by using a herbicide or by hoeing, though in established rows hoeing is likely to disturb the surface roots. A mulch applied in May will do nothing but good – as well as providing additional food it will retain moisture and keep down weeds. Sprinkle a general fertilizer along each side of the row in February or March and again in late July or early August after pruning. A rose fertilizer, rich in potash, is ideal for this.

Ensure that the crop is given adequate supplies of water in dry weather.

As soon as the fruits start to form the canes should be draped with fine mesh string or plastic netting, otherwise birds will take the majority of the fruits.

Propagation

Raspberries are very easy to propagate. Simply dig up healthy suckers, severing them from the parent plant, and insert them in late autumn to form a new plantation. Dig up and replant any plantation about every five years – preferably moving it to another site to avoid the recurrence of pest and disease attack.

Harvesting

Pick the fruits, leaving the core behind, as soon as they are fully coloured and will part readily from the plant.

Storing. Varieties which will freeze well are recommended under the list of selected varieties. On that there is nothing further to say except that you might be surprised at how fresh they taste when brought from the freezer and served with cream in the middle of winter!

Pests and diseases

Raspberries are subject to quite a few pests and diseases and the ones you are most likely to encounter are aphids, raspberry beetle, raspberry moth and raspberry cane midge. Diseases which may be troublesome are cane blight, cane spot, spur blight and botrytis.

For controls see pages 120 to 123.

Malling Exploit, an excellent variety which crops well and is useful for freezing

Strawberries

Strawberries and summer always seem to be synonymous and maybe this is why so many of us like to grow and eat this fruit.

Selected varieties

Strawberry varieties fall into two principal groups: those fruiting in the main season, June and July; and the perpetual or remontant, cropping from summer well into the autumn.

Good varieties of the first group are Cambridge Vigour, Cambridge Late Pine, Gorella, Redgauntlet, Tamella (especially useful for producing early crops under cloches), Grandee, Cambridge Favourite (and my own favourite) and, of course, Royal Sovereign. Unfortunately, although to my mind the last is the finest flavoured variety, it is extremely difficult to obtain virus-free stock of it, and even if you do then the plants quickly become infected and this reduces the crop to twenty-five per cent. or less of what it should be.

Remontant varieties include Gento, Sonjano, Sans Rivale and Triplex.

Growing from seed to crop in the same year the alpine strawberries make an interesting variation and Baron Solemacher is the one to try.

Strawberries need some form of protection to keep them away from the soil. Straw is traditionally used but bituminised mats or polythene are good alternatives

Pot-grown strawberries should be planted so that the top of the root ball is slightly below the level of the soil's surface

Soil and situation

In order to get one's money's worth from strawberries, they must be grown quickly, without any check, which is no easy task if the spring is dry and the summer hot. Much depends on good soil management and whilst the chosen site needs to be well drained the soil must also be moisture retentive.

Soil preparation, therefore, is all important and my practice is to dig the ground to a depth of about 25 cm (10 in), digging in manure and removing all perennial weeds at the same time. This needs to be done a month to six weeks before planting to give the soil time to settle. Then immediately before planting I sprinkle bonemeal and a general fertilizer over the surface at the rate of a handful to the square metre (square yard).

Plants

Once you have made the all-important decision about which varieties to grow then you must obtain the plants and, in the first instance anyway, I do advise you to buy virus-free certified stock from a specialist grower.

Planting

Planting should be done before the end of September to allow time for the plants to get established and build up good root systems and crowns before the weather turns cold. Such plants will fruit well the following summer. If the planting has to be left until October or November then the plants will be correspondingly smaller and will have to be deblossomed the following spring as there will not be sufficient growth to support a crop.

The autumn-fruiting varieties, however, can be planted in the spring for fruiting in the same year.

When it comes to the method of planting, dip any plants with dry roots in water, then plant firmly with the crowns level with the soil surface; in the case of container-grown plants then the soil ball should be set just below the level of the ground. Space the plants 45 to 60 cm (18 to 24 in) apart in rows 75 cm ($2\frac{1}{2}$ ft) apart. Water well.

Cultivation

My first task in spring is to clean up the beds and then to give a sprinkling of fertilizer. For this I like to use a rose fertilizer because of its extra potash and magnesium content.

Water well throughout the season whenever the weather is dry. When the fruits start to form some sort of protection should be put down, this can be straw, bituminised paper mats or straw mats. Black polythene is also used but it is important not to put this down until the beginning of June because of the danger of late frost. In the event of this happening the polythene keeps the warmth in the ground and a layer of moisture collects on the underside, this in turn has a tendency to draw the frost and damage the flowers and fruits.

Remove any runners not required for propagation, doing this frequently throughout the summer. If left on they will reduce the plants' fruiting capacity in the following year.

Spraying is an important part of the growing programme and I give several applications of a systemic insecticide from the early part of the year until the fruits begin to form.

Birds are a major menace and the plants will need some form of protection; a fruit cage is the best but netting spread over the rows is also effective.

After harvesting, the straw,

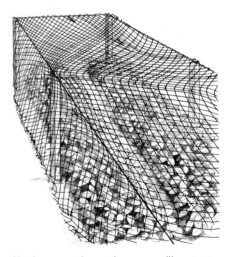

Netting, spread over the rows, will protect the fruit from bird attack

polythene, or mats should be removed and the beds weeded and cleaned up, all surplus runners and old growth being pulled off. Finally a feed of general fertilizer is applied.

The useful life of a strawberry plant is three years and after this plants should be scrapped and new ones put in. What I do is to plant two rows each year and pull up two rows each year, so I always have three-year, two-year and one-year-old plants on the go.

Growing under cloches

By making use of cloches it is possible to have fruit ripe a month earlier than the normal outdoor crop. I usually put the cloches over a row of second-year plants in March. On warm days when the plants are in flower, it is a good idea to remove the cloches temporarily.

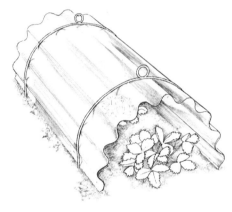

Cloches can be used to ripen an early crop of fruit

Propagation

It is possible to raise your own plants from existing stock by layering the runners. Choose strong, healthy plants and allow four to six runners to form on each. At the beginning of July peg the first plantlets on each runner into 8-cm (3-in) pots of John Innes potting compost No. 1. The pots are plunged into the soil around each stock plant. The layers will have formed roots in August and can be detached and planted out.

Because of the presence of so much virus in strawberries it is important to renew your beds periodically with certified stock.

Increasing strawberries by pegging the runners into small pots of compost

Growing strawberries in pots

I make a point of having the first strawberries ripe in pots at the end of April and they normally continue right through until we get the outside crop. For growing in this way I use Cambridge Favourite and it is essential to get the runners layered in July. When the layers are well rooted, which should be before the end of August, they are potted up in threes in 15- or 18-cm (6- or 7-in) pots using John Innes potting compost No. 3. When potting, the compost must be rammed in with a rammer to make sure it is firm. The pots are then stood out of doors and watered as necessary.

In late January move them first into a cool greenhouse, and then into a warmer one as the leaves begin to grow, and from this point feed weekly with a liquid tomato fertilizer. Select ten or twelve

To support the fruits above the pot place a cane in each side and twist raffia around the stems and between the canes

flowers on each plant and pick the others off. When the fruits form they will need supporting with raffia and canes to keep them above the pot and the compost so that they will stay dry during watering.

Strawberries grown in this way will still need spraying regularly to keep them free from aphid.

Strawberries can be grown in a range of containers or barrels out of doors and as such not only make a decorative feature for the patio but also provide quite a good crop of fruit. Use John Innes potting compost No. 3 to fill the container.

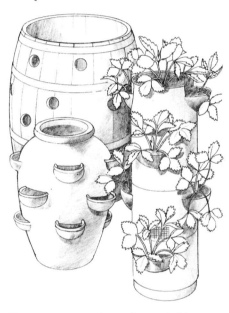

There are a range of containers suitable for growing strawberries. A barrel with holes drilled in the sides, a strawberry pot and tower pots are shown here

Harvesting and storing

Pick when the fruits are fully ripe and dry, taking the calyx as well. Strawberries can be stored by freezing although they are not the best fruit for this. Bottling and jam making are other ways of preserving them.

Pests and diseases

The worst pest is the aphid, closely followed by slugs and birds. Red spider mite may also be a problem.

As I mentioned earlier viruses can be very troublesome. Other diseases are grey mould, or botrytis, and mildew. See pages 120 to 123.

Pests and Diseases of Fruit Crops

Safety Precautions

All chemicals should be applied strictly according to the manufacturer's instructions and protective clothing worn if recommended.

It is especially important to observe the periods of time which must be allowed to elapse between the applications of the insecticide and fungicide and the harvesting of the crops.

Keep all chemicals out of the reach of children and away from animals, and wash out all spraying apparatus after use.

Pest	Crops Attacked	Symptoms and Damage Caused	Control
Aphids	Almost all crops are attacked by various aphids. Sometimes a particular kind of aphid will only attack one specific crop; for example mealy plum aphid.	Honeydew is secreted on to the foliage which also becomes discoloured and distorted. Virus diseases are transmitted by aphids.	The overwintering eggs are effectively destroyed by tar oil winter washes. Spray in summer with gamma HCH*, derris, malathion or dimethoate.
Apple blossom weevil	Apple	The centre of the flower and the stamens are eaten away and the rest of the flower turns brown. No fruit is set.	Spray with malathion in spring and apply a tar oil wash in winter.
Apple sawfly	Apple	Apples frequently bear a curved 'S'-shaped brown scar. Maggots burrow into the apples in June and excrete unpleasant-smelling frass (the pulped apple flesh).	Spray with dimethoate or HCH* one week after petal fall.
Apple sucker	Apple and pear	Small, aphid-like insects suck the sap from the plant and so reduce the vigour.	Spray in winter with a tar oil wash to kill the eggs. Spray with dimethoate or malathion at the pink or white bud and petal fall stages.
Big bud mite	Black currant	Buds become fat and swollen. The mite carries the reversion virus of black currants.	Spray with lime sulphur in spring, except on the sulphur-shy variety Wellington XXX which should be pruned free of the pest. Other sulphur-shy varieties are Davidson's Eight, Edina, Goliath and Victoria. These varieties can be sprayed with malathion.
Birds	A wide range. Cherries and cane fruits are particularly susceptible.	Fruits and blossoms are partially eaten or destroyed.	Fruit cages are the best solution. Bird scarers are rarely effective, though the cotton-like 'Scaraweb' which is strewn over the trees is quite a good deterrent.
Brown scale	Gooseberry, fig and occasionally other crops.	Small, brown, dome-shaped scales fasten themselves to the stems and branches where they suck the sap. The vigour of attacked plants is reduced.	Spray in winter with a tar oil wash, and during the growing season with systemic insecticide.
Capsid bug	A wide range of crops are affected, but in particular apples, pears, black and red currants.	Leaves are punctured and spotted. Apple and pear fruits develop small, brown, raised areas of a corky texture and can become distorted.	Spray in winter with a tar oil wash or in summer with gamma HCH*.
Codling moth	Apple	Fruits contain maggots which can usually be seen to have entered by the stalk of the fruit. No unpleasant smell is emitted by the fruit and the attack usually takes place after June in contrast to the apple sawfly.	Spray in winter with a tar oil wash; or with malathion in mid-June and again in early July.
Gooseberry red spider mite	Gooseberry	The sap is sucked by the mites and the leaves become yellow and may eventually fall off. Fruits are also shed before they are fully developed.	Spray in February with DNOC or in summer with derris or malathion.
Gooseberry sawfly	Gooseberry	Leaves are eaten by the caterpillars of the sawfly. Bushes can be stripped within a few days in a severe attack.	Spray with malathion or derris.

Pest	Crops Attacked	Symptoms and Damage Caused	Control
Leather jackets	Strawberry	The base of the stem and the roots are eaten away.	Fork into the soil an insecticide containing gamma HCH*.
Mealy bug	Fig, grape and occasionally other crops	Small bugs coated with woolly looking white wax are visible on the stems and leaves where they suck the sap.	Spray with malathion or petroleum oil in summer, and with a tar oil wash in winter, or systemic insecticide early in the year.
Mussel scale	Apples	Dark grey scales, like minute mussel shells, sit tightly on the twigs and branches, sucking the sap and reducing the vigour of the tree.	Spray in winter with a tar oil wash and with a systemic insecticide early in the year.
Pear leaf blister mite	Pears and occasionally plums	Leaves become puckered, develop red blisters and eventually fall. Fruits may develop small scabby areas.	Spray with DNOC in winter and 5% lime sulphur in March just before the buds open.
Pear midge	Pear	Maggots attack the young fruitlets causing them to swell rapidly and eventually to fall to the ground in June and July.	Spray with DNOC between bud burst and white bud.
Plum sawfly	Plum	The fruits contain maggots and will be gummed and often distorted.	Spray with dimethoate one week after petal fall.
Raspberry beetle	Raspberry, loganberry and blackberry	Maggots are found inside the fruits and can often ruin the whole crop.	Spray with derris at petal fall and again 2 weeks later
Raspberry cane midge	Raspberry	The midge burrows into the young canes. It is undesirable as it allows the entry of cane blight.	Spray with gamma HCH* in early and mid-May.
Raspberry moth	Raspberry	Caterpillars bore into the lateral shoots in early spring. When the shoots are about 2·5 cm (1 in) long they wilt and die.	Remove and burn infected shoots. Spray with a tar oil wash in winter.
Red spider mite	Apples, peaches, plums and occasionally other crops	Bleaching and curling of the leaves and a reduction in vigour. In severe cases a thin grey web will envelop the leaves and tips of shoots. The mites are the size of pin-pricks and reddish brown in colour.	Spray in February with DNOC or in summer with derris or malathion.
Shot-hole borer	Plum	Small, round holes caused by beetles will be found in branches and young stems. The tree wilts and in a severe attack may die.	Remove and burn all infected branches. Paint all cuts with a bituminous wound dressing.
Slugworm	Pears and cherries	Leaves are eaten by small, brown caterpillars; often only the veins of the leaves are left intact.	Spray with derris.
Slugs and snails	Strawberry	Leaves, flowers and stem bases are eaten away.	Poisoned baits and pellets can be placed under a tile or in a short length of drainpipe out of reach of children and animals.
Strawberry eelworm	Strawberry	Various symptoms including death of the central crown of the plant, puckering and distortion of the leaves. The symptoms are most prevalent in May.	Dig up and burn infected plants. Avoid growing strawberries on land known to be infected.
Tarsonemid mite	Strawberry	Foliage becomes bleached, brown and wrinkled. The fruits are small and there is a great reduction in vigour. The mites may be seen under a hand lens.	Spray with lime sulphur at winter strength in April or systemic insecticide early in the year.
Tortrix moth	Apple	Leaves and the surface of the fruit are eaten. A leaf is often stuck to the damaged part of the fruit. Leaves are occasionally spun together to contain the larvae.	Spray in winter with a DNOC wash or later in the season with HCH*.
Winter moth	Apples, cherries, pears and plums	Leaves, shoots, flowers and fruits are eaten by the caterpillars of the moth.	The moths can be trapped on grease bands wrapped around the trunk of the tree from September to March. Eggs can be destroyed by tar oil winter washes applied between December and March. Gamma HCH* can be applied at the green and pink or white bud stages.
Woolly aphid (American blight)	A wide range of top fruit crops	Reduction in vigour and transmission of virus diseases. This pest is easily recognized by the white, woolly covering which will be spread over the whole colony.	Spray in winter with a tar oil wash. Spray in June with malathion giving 2 applications and allowing 2 weeks to elapse between sprays.

*formerly BHC

Disease	Crops Attacked	Symptoms and Damage Caused	Control
Bacterial canker	Plum and cherry	Gummy, sunken areas are evident on the trunk or branches of the tree. The leaves may develop yellow spots which eventually become holes. Individual branches wilt and the whole tree may wilt and die.	Graft trees on to resistant rootstocks such as F12/1 for cherries, and Myrobalan B for plums. Remove all infected wood and spray trees with Bordeaux mixture in late August, mid-September and early October.
Bitter pit	Apple and pear	Small, brown sunken areas develop in the fruits and the flesh at these areas turns brown.	This is not a disease but a disorder which is caused by irregular sap flow, due in turn to irregular supplies of water. Ensure that adequate water is available at all times and choose resistant varieties if this disorder is frequently encountered. See also p. 87.
Black currant leaf spot	Black, red, and white currant	Black areas develop on the leaves and spread until, eventually, the leaves drop off.	Spray with zineb after flowering and again in May, June and after the fruit has been picked.
Blossom wilt	Apple, cherry, pear and plum	Blossoms and young shoot tips wilt and die. Cankers form on the blossom spurs and spread to the branches.	Cut out and burn infected wood. Spray with tar oil in winter.
Botrytis (grey mould)	Strawberry, raspberry and fig.	In strawberries, flowers and foliage turn brown and rotten and are covered with a greyish fur. The crown may rot off completely. In raspberries just the fruit is affected by mould in damp weather.	Space the plants adequately and avoid keeping them excessively wet. Spray with benomyl, captan or thiram.
Brown rot	Apple, apricot, pear and plum	The symptoms of this disease are many and varied. Flowers and young shoots wilt and small cankers develop on the stems. The most characteristic damage appears on the fruit which turns brown and rotten and develops concentric white rings of fungal growth. It is particularly damaging in fruit stores where it can spread from infected to uninfected fruits.	Remove dead or dying wood from the trees. Spray with captan at 3-week intervals from early July to late September. Collect and destroy all affected fruits in late summer and early autumn.
Cane blight	Raspberry	Canes become brittle and die in spring, snapping off easily at the base. Wilting of young growth. Cankers are visible beneath cracked bark at the base of the stems.	Remove and burn infected canes. Keep down raspberry cane midge.
Cane spot	Raspberries and loganberries	Dark purple spots appear on young canes; these turn into sunken and splitting cankers as the canes age. Growth is stunted, vigour reduced and cropping is badly affected.	Spray with benomyl or with lime sulphur at twice the winter strength in March.
Canker	Apples and pears are attacked by one kind of canker, figs by another.	The bark flakes off and cracks. Sunken and shrivelled wounds appear on the branches.	Ensure an adequate supply of nutrients is available to the tree. Cut out and burn infected tissue, painting the cuts with a bituminous wound dressing.
Coral spot	Red and white currant. Also dead or dying wood on other fruit trees	Raised orange spots appear on dead or dying wood and hasten the death of living tissue.	Prune out dead or diseased wood and treat cuts with a bituminous wound dressing.
Die back	Apricot, cherry, gooseberry, peach, plum and red currant	Flower trusses wilt and die and the infection – caused by a fungus – may spread down the stems and kill out whole branches of the bush or tree.	Cut out and burn infected wood. Paint all cuts with a bituminous wound dressing.
Fireblight	Apples, pears and other members of the rose family but not plums	The disease enters through the blossom which wilts and dies. Infection spreads backwards causing death of leaves and stems. The leaves turn brown and whole branches look as though they have been damaged by fire. Orange-brown stains are visible beneath the bark. Individual branches die and, if the infection is not caught soon enough, the whole tree can be destroyed.	Remove and burn all diseased wood cutting well back into healthy tissue. Paint cuts with a bituminous wound dressing. Grub out and burn badly infected trees.
Mildew	Apples, peaches, grapes and strawberries are attacked by different types. The gooseberry is attacked by two distinct kinds.	White powdery deposits appear on the leaves – particularly at the shoot tips. Growths become spindly and weak.	Spray with dinocap. Gooseberry mildew can be controlled by spraying with lime sulphur as soon as the fruits set and again 3 weeks later.

Disease	Crops Attacked	Symptoms and Damage Caused	Control
Peach leaf curl	Peach and nectarine	The leaves become curled and puckered and develop bright red blisters. The leaves are shed and the vigour of the plant is reduced.	Spray with Bordeaux mixture in late February or early March as the buds begin to swell.
Red core	Strawberry	The plants wilt and on being dug up the roots will be found to be like mouse tails. A red streak will be found down the centre of the root if it is cut with a knife.	Dig up and burn infected plants. Grow resistant varieties. Ensure that the ground in which the strawberries are grown is well drained as this disease is prominent in waterlogged soil.
Reversion	Black currant	A serious disease causing the leaves to be coarsely toothed and reducing the number of veins. Cropping is greatly reduced or completely prevented. This virus disease is carried by the big bud mite.	Burn infected bushes. Propagate from clean, healthy stock and spray against big bud mite.
Rust	Black currant and plum	Brown or orange powdery spots appear on the undersides of the leaves in summer. Vigour is reduced.	Spray frequently with zineb.
Scab	Apple and pear	Leaves develop black blotches in summer. The fruits become blotched with sunken, scabby patches which eventually crack open ruining the fruits.	Spray with captan from petal fall onwards.
Silver leaf	Plum, and occasionally peach, nectarine and cherry	Vigour is reduced and the leaves become silvery in appearance. Infected branches, when cut, will have a dark brown discolouration in the wood. Infection will eventually spread to the whole tree if not dealt with promptly.	Remove all infected wood by 15th July and seal the cuts with a bituminous wound dressing. Avoid damaging the trees and so allowing the disease to enter. The variety Victoria is particularly susceptible.
Spur blight	Raspberry and loganberry	Purplish blotches at the bases of the leaves eventually turn into greyish-white cracks and spread along the canes. Buds in the infected area die but the canes remain alive. Infection can be given a foothold by the damage of raspberry cane midge.	Cut out and burn infected canes. Control raspberry cane midge.
Virus diseases	Many crops	The symptoms are many and varied and can produce mottled, distorted and wrinkled leaves and deformed or oddly coloured flowers. Vigour is greatly reduced and plants wilt and occasionally die.	Dig up and burn infected plants. Keep down aphids and other pests which transmit these diseases.
Witches broom	Cherry	Bushy, broom-like growths caused by a fungal infection develop on the branches. These sap vigour from the rest of the tree and do not produce any fruit themselves.	Cut out and burn all 'brooms' and paint the cuts with a bituminous wound dressing.